The Guide Owning an
Oriental
Shorthair Cat

Lynn Miller

CONTENTS

All photos by Isabelle Francais except the following: Julie Keyer (pages 27, 29), Roy Keyer (page 30), Barbara Levine (pages 5, 42), Lynn Miller (pages 9, 13, 14, 31, 35 [top], 36, 37 [top and bottom], 38, 39, 40, 43, 54, 56, 57, 58).

The publisher thanks the following owners of cats pictured in this book: Gloria and Susan Adler; Richard and Lori Bilello; James J. Bushey and Robert H. Solomon; Karen Christmann; Carol Fogarty; Lisa M. Greco and Pat Wardell; Christy Harden; Patricia Hopkins; Cher Kelly; Julie and Roy Keyer; Barbara Levine; Dean Mastrangelo; Lynn, Victor, and Rachel Miller; Cleora Scott.

RE 414

Distributed in the UNITED STATES to the Pet Trade by T.F.H. Publications, Inc., 1 TFH Plaza, Neptune City, NJ 07753; on the Internet at www.tfh.com; in CANADA by Rolf C. Hagen Inc., 3225 Sartelon St., Montreal, Quebec H4R 1E8; Pet Trade by H & L Pet Supplies Inc., 27 Kingston Crescent, Kitchener, Ontario N2B 2T6; in ENGLAND by T.F.H. Publications, PO Box 74, Havant PO9 5TT; in AUSTRALIA AND THE SOUTH PACIFIC by T.F.H. (Australia), Pty. Ltd., Box 149, Brookvale 2100 N.S.W., Australia; in NEW ZEALAND by Brooklands Aquarium Ltd., 5 McGiven Drive, New Plymouth, RD1 New Zealand; in SOUTH AFRICA by Rolf C. Hagen S.A. (PTY.) LTD., P.O. Box 201199, Durban North 4016, South Africa; in JAPAN by T.F.H. Publications. Published by T.F.H. Publications, Inc.

MANUFACTURED IN THE
UNITED STATES OF AMERICA
BY T.F.H. PUBLICATIONS, INC.

INTRODUCTION: WHAT IS AN ORIENTAL SHORTHAIR?

What is an Oriental? It is a cat that was created as an idea—a creative effort by different groups of people in different countries at different times using the tools nature had provided. The first "Oriental" that I remember seeing was in a cat book in early 1973, and the cat was called a Foreign Shorthair. I thought that it was beautiful, but there were none that I knew of in the United States.

Not long afterwards, I was at a friend's house with several other Siamese breeders, and we began to talk about the possibilities of importing some of these cats from England. After some correspondence, we discovered that there were breeders in England and Holland who would help us get started.

I owned one of the first kittens imported from England to begin Orientals in the US. It was so exciting, because people all over the world were interested and were watching us. We exhibited them at many shows, talked about them, formed a breed club, and wrote about them. We also contacted breeders and owners of other Foreign Shorthairs in the US.

The Oriental Shorthair is now among the most popular breeds in the world. It is a cat with the Siamese personality and Siamese type, but with dozens of possible coat colors and patterns.

The breed standard was written with the help of some of the top geneticists in the world. It was based on the Siamese standard with just a few words changed but many colors and patterns were added. The best Siamese cats in the world were used to breed the beautiful Orientals that were being born, and we were able to show them in competition quickly.

The Oriental Shorthair was created on paper with a very high standard in mind. Many of the Orientals being shown today have just about met that standard. Colors and patterns have been added, and the Oriental is now among the most popular breeds in the world. The breeders are intelligent and revise the standard often as more is learned about genetics and health.

The Oriental is much like the cat that we hoped it would be—a cat with the Siamese personality and Siamese type, but with so many colors and patterns. They are "talkers" just like their Siamese relatives. They are still allowed to be bred to Siamese and often are. Many Oriental breeders are also Siamese breeders.

Sharing your life with an Oriental is an experience that is hard to describe. Every move you make will be supervised by your loving feline friend. Whether it is loading the dishwasher, brushing your teeth, or folding clean clothes—you will not be alone! An Oriental will learn your behavior and anticipate every move. From the time the alarm clock goes off in the morning until you turn off the lights at night, she will be by your side.

Some of their favorite activities are helping to fold laundry (as long as they get to sit on the warm clothes), sitting on top of your computer and playing with the cursor on the screen, and rushing to see who gets to the vents first when they hear the heat come on. Orientals love the heat. By day, they will find the sunniest spots by the windows and doors. The warmth of computers, microwaves, ovens, and dishwashers attracts them.

An Oriental's life is not complete until she has climbed up as high as your ceiling. Most kitchens are arranged to make

Active, talkative, and extremely intelligent, Oriental Shorthairs like Patipause Majimece (an ebony ticked tabby) need lots of attention. Daily play sessions will help keep them out of mischief.

Oriental cats love their people, but they also enjoy other felines. Here, GC, RW Felitan Mick Jaguar of Y-Not drapes an affectionate paw around his best buddy, GP Algebra's Calypso of Y-Not.

this an easy task by jumping onto the counter and then the refrigerator. Just think of those long arms, legs, and body stretching up as high as possible to touch the ceiling. Of course, there is the "moving ladder" trick, also—beware of the perimeter of the room when an Oriental cat is on your shoulder. If you are near a bookcase, wall unit, or any tall piece of furniture, one jump and she is on top of it—just like she planned to be.

Any toy of yours will be attractive to your cat. You may not think of your spoon, hairbrush, shoes, pens, remote control, or socks as toys—but guess what? Your furry feline will have other ideas. Just like she will want to taste all of your foods, not knowing why she cannot, she will consider all of your things to be fun for her.

Oriental cats love their people, but they also enjoy other felines. The choice between sitting with you or a pile of their pals is a difficult decision for them to make. Of course, if you pull a special toy out of a hiding place, *all* of them will join you.

Many of them will "talk" to you and really try to carry on a conversation. Most will learn their names at a very young age and come when called. This does not mean that the cat that knows her name will not hide from you on occasion. At about the time when you've looked under every bed, on every chair, behind furniture, checked cabinets in the kitchen and

To an Oriental Shorthair like cinnamon-colored Ch. Patipause Colorance 7RB, exploring the house, running and jumping, and climbing furniture is all in a day's work.

bathroom, retraced your steps many times, and wondered when the cat could have escaped, she will appear in the middle of the room and just look at you as if to say, "I'm never telling."

Orientals are an active breed of cat. They do not just sit around waiting for you to get home. They are too busy exploring everything. They run.

They jump. They climb. They will greet all of your friends and entertain them with their antics. You will learn to put things in drawers, on high shelves, and behind closed doors. You will probably cringe when someone brings you a bouquet of flowers or a plant, because even if it's poisonous, it's still a cat toy to them. How to enjoy flowers on top of a bookcase, in the basement, or on the front porch should be taught in a course entitled "Living with a Cat 101."

Some other dangers are paper clips, safety pins, sewing needles, thread, yarn, string, ribbon, scissors, knives, razors, rubber bands, tops of cans, single pipe cleaners, dental floss, cotton swabs, cotton balls, broken glass, sharp things, little things, rocking chairs, recliners, sofa beds, hi-risers, open windows, fireplaces, ledges, lofts...and the list goes on. One can never be too careful. Accidents do happen, but so many can be prevented. Needless to say, the Oriental is not meant to lead an outdoor kind of life. She is intended to live indoors as a pampered pet.

Children and Oriental cats become great friends and will "talk" to each other for hours. Some Oriental cats love being the center of attention (at times) and will help play with dolls, tea parties, blocks, and even dress-up. Some will claim certain dolls or soft animals as theirs and will take them everywhere with them. Of course your Oriental will also want to help do jigsaw puzzles, play board games, and even step on the remote control to change the channel on the TV.

An Oriental cat will be your best friend, because you can tell her anything. She will listen and pretend to understand. She will be there for you and expect you to be there for her. She will live for many years and want to share every moment of your life with you.

REFERENCES AND SUGGESTED READING

Most of the history of the breed in this book is from memory along with articles in *The Cat Fanciers Association* [CFA] *Yearbook* by Vicky Markstein (1978) and Heather Lorimer (1992 and 1996). One of my favorite books, and the book where I viewed an Oriental (then called a Foreign Shorthair) for the first time is Grace Pond's *The Complete Cat Encyclopedia.* Richard Gebhardt's *The Complete Cat Book* tells about the Oriental and some of the history. Unfortunately, there is very little written history about the Oriental. There have been magazine articles over the years that were usually not well received by Oriental breeders upon publication, and I did not review them for this book. Robert Agresta, CFA Breed Council Secretary for many years, was very helpful in sharing articles, tables, and facts with me.

Breeding Pedigreed Cats, by Carolyn Vella and John J. McGonagle, Jr., is a book that anyone thinking about breeding cats should read. Although we own two versions of Roy Robinson's *Genetics for Cat Breeders*, I could not resist buying the newest *Robinson's Genetics for Cat Breeders & Veterinarians*. It is so much easier to understand, with a wonderful glossary and chapters about anomalies, color genetics, tables, and much more. Carolyn M. Vella, Lorraine M. Shelton, John J. McGonagle, Jr., and Terry W. Stanglein wrote the fourth edition in 1999, and I highly recommend it.

HISTORY OF THE ORIENTAL SHORTHAIR

It all began with the Siamese. Independently, in different parts of the world, people started to imagine Siamese cats "painted" in different colors. From accidental breedings to extremely planned, scientific breedings, Siamese were being created in different colors. Several had different names and breeds until they were joined together in the mid-1970s as Oriental Shorthairs:

CHESTNUT/HAVANA

The first known "self-brown" cat (meaning that the fur was a solid color from root to tip) was called Granny Grumps. She belonged to pioneer English cat fancier Mrs. French in 1894. In 1923, there were reports of brown "foreign" cats called "Swiss Mountain Cats" in continental Europe. In 1951, three serious breeders studied the chocolate (brown) gene inheritance in cats and planned a breeding program to create a self-chocolate cat of foreign type. In 1952, the famous Elmtower Bronze Idol, a self-chocolate male kitten, was born. Laurentide Brown Prior was born in 1953, and along with two other male

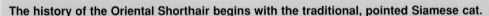

The history of the Oriental Shorthair begins with the traditional, pointed Siamese cat.

All over the world, cat fanciers began to imagine Siamese cats "painted" in different colors. Through both accidental breedings and careful planning, this soon became a reality.

kittens, became the foundation of the Havana in England.

The Havana was given full recognition in 1958 after three generations of like-to-like breeding. The new breed was called Chestnut Brown Foreign Shorthair to differentiate it from the Havana rabbit. In 1970, the Governing Council of the Cat Fancy (GCCF), the premier cat organization in England, agreed to use the name Havana again. Crossways Honeysuckle Rose was the first champion Havana in the early 1960s.

In 1956, Roofspringer Mahogany (female) and Laurentide Brown Pilgrim (male) were the first to be exported to the US, where they were called Havana Browns. In 1974, when the Foreign Shorthairs/Orientals were being developed in the US, most of the Havana Browns were re-registered as Orientals.

LAVENDERS

Lavender Oriental Shorthairs were first known as Foreign Lavender or Foreign Lilac. Praha Allegro Agitato was shown in England in the 1950s, but it was not until the late 1960s that a few breeders set up a serious breeding program. Mrs. Angela

Sayer and Mrs. Betty Harrison worked with two different lines to reach GCCF recognition with as little inbreeding as possible. In 1970, Mallorca Li-Ming was Best in Show and her daughter Solitaire Lavendula (a Sayer Cat) was best kitten at the Gwynedd Cat Club's first show.

Photos of Mrs. Sayer's Solitaire Amethyst can be seen in many cat books. In Grace Pond's *Encyclopedia of the Cat*, the author states, "Harislau Echo, Eloise, and Estralita [bred by Betty Harrison] will be invaluable in the development of the breed." She was correct, because some of the first Orientals imported into

Lavender cats like GC, NW Chromatics Amethyst and Chromatics Cartier were first known in the 1960s and early 1970s as Foreign Lavender or Foreign Lilac. In 1974, lavenders were re-registered as Oriental Shorthairs.

Havana Browns are self-brown cats of foreign type that were developed over the course of the 20th century. Most are now registered as Orientals in the United States.

the US were from Harrison/Sayer lines and many Orientals have these cats in their pedigrees.

There were some lavenders in the US in the late 1960s and early 1970s. Mrs. Ann Billheimer of Florida bred one of them, Grand Champion Tawnee Ballerina. They never advanced beyond registration status in the CFA and were also re-registered as Oriental Shorthairs in 1974.

FOREIGN WHITE

Grace Pond described the Foreign White as "merely a Siamese wearing a white overcoat as a disguise." This is because the gene for white fur is dominant and will mask the color(s) underneath. One can guess as to what those other colors are, but only test breedings will be the proof.

Foreign Whites were developed in the UK in the 1960s. These white Orientals were first imported to the United States in the mid-1970s.

Again, three breeders had independent thoughts about the creation of a white cat with foreign type. The year was 1962, and the breeders were Miss Pat Turner and Mr. Brian Stirling-Webb from England and Miss Elizabeth Flack of Northern Ireland. They did not meet until 1964, when they were told about each other. They first called the cats Chinese White, but changed this to Foreign White Cat. They became affiliated with the GCCF in 1971.

The beginning Foreign White breeders claim that they only used the very best cats in their breeding programs. They neutered or spayed cats with green and odd-colored eyes (meaning two eyes of different colors), not knowing that they would be accepted today in the show ring. They were also very careful to weed out the lines with hereditary deafness.

The first white Oriental imported into the US was probably (White) Rigodon van Batn el Bakarah, a blue-eyed white male that produced white Orientals in the late 1970s.

TABBIES

In early Oriental pedigrees, one can see the word "Mau" as a breed. These were either spotted or mackerel tabby, patterned on a paler body color. Mrs. Angela Sayer bred them to good-quality Siamese and Havanas to maintain type. Several were imported to the US in 1974, and they were important to the history of the Oriental cat.

PIONEER BREEDERS IN THE UNITED STATES

In the 1960s, Irene Gizzi was working with ebony and red Orientals on the west coast of the US. Mrs. Betty Pursglove was also working with other colors in Michigan. Other early Oriental breeders were Judy Broadbent, Marjorie Jordan, Lynn Lamoreux, Sid and Pauline

Tabby cats of foreign body type, once called "Mau," are important to the history of the Oriental Shorthair. Glor-ee Esmeralda is just one result of this influential heritage.

Thompson, John Smith, and Dorothy and Donald Wilbur.

Vicky Markstein, writing in the *CFA Yearbook,* describes the Oriental Shorthair pioneers as "starting with the man-made standard for the Siamese cat without the color pattern. ...the entire spectrum of colors offered by nature would be used to enrich the breed." After much research, Vicky and her husband Peter realized that the only way to register the Orientals in the CFA would be as a single breed. They thought that the most difficult part would be to convince at least ten breeders to pledge their interest.

They invited Siamese breeders in the New York area to their home, talked to them and showed them photos. Many agreed to work with the breed by importing cats from England. Within two weeks, there were almost 20 potential breeders. Most of them had never seen an Oriental except in books and photographs. It was very exciting to create a standard and a breed club for an abstract cat, and it was done in record time.

The club was originally called Foreign Shorthairs International, but this was changed to Oriental Shorthairs International prior to submitting a CFA application. The charter members were the late William Eisenman (CFA judge), the late Barbara Harr, the late Alison Hedberg, Judith Hymas Thomas (CFA judge), Richard and Barbara Levitan, Anthony Marescie, Barbara Marescie (Levine), Peter and Vicky Markstein (now TICA judges),

Jeoffrey and Gail Miles, Bob O'Brien, Joan O'Brien (Singer), Ann Tacetta, Lou Weiss, Lynn Hirschfeld Weiss (Miller), and Donald and Dorothy Wilbur. Other breeders were invited to join the pioneers.

In February 1974, Oriental kittens from England started to arrive: Solitaire Keleawe (chestnut), Harislau Magnolia and Harislau Myosotis (spotted lavenders), Solitaire Tut (chestnut spotted tabby), and Scintilla Tangent (cream). Alice's Sakura and Solitaire Tongan Princess (Chestnut females), already imported by Sid and Pauline Thompson, were "added" to the original group. Vicky Markstein states in her 1978 *CFA Yearbook* article, "Since eight of CFA's first ten OSH grand champions have these imports in their pedigrees, the overseas breeders made significant contributions to the USA Oriental development."

Orientals are now accepted and shown all over the world, in all cat registry associations. Here, GP Y-Not the Beat Goes On, an ebony tabby, is being judged at a Cat Fanciers' Association show.

ORIENTALS ON EXHIBIT

In 1974, in White Plains, New York, Orientals were shown for the first time in the US, as an exhibition only. Registration was granted in October 1974, and provisional breed status was granted in October 1975 (effective May 1, 1976). In October 1976, Orientals were advanced in all of the colors to full championship status, effective May 1, 1977.

CFA's first Oriental Shorthair grand champion was tortoiseshell female Patapaw Justa Foo-Lin, bred and owned by Marilyn Buchanan. Grand Champion Sand N'Sea Bikkuri of Jemwyck, a lavender spotted tabby female, was the first Oriental Shorthair on the CFA's top 20 list in 1977. She was bred by Alison U. Hedberg and owned by Jayne E. Murray.

Prior to CFA's acceptance of Orientals, the Cat Fanciers' Federation (CFF) granted them championship status. The first Oriental grand champion was Lolytin's The Pharoah of Faro, bred by Lynn Weiss and owned by Ethel DuBois.

Orientals are now accepted all over the world in all cat registry associations. In 1998–1999, they were the sixth most popular breed of cat in the CFA, and the eighth most popular in the GCCF.

THE ORIENTAL SHORTHAIR STANDARD AND COLORS

An Oriental is long, muscular, surprisingly heavy, and tubular. These are all words that have described this wonderful breed over the years. They have been called the "Greyhounds of the Cat Fancy." The head should be wedge-shaped, beginning at the muzzle and finishing with the tips of the large, wide-set ears. A long, straight profile is required. The tip of the chin should line up with the tip of the nose. Eyes should be slanted and almond-shaped. Green eyes are preferred, although Orientals have been known to have blue, yellow, or turquoise eyes. White Orientals may have blue, green, or odd-eyed eye color.

The body should be tubular, with the hips the same size as the shoulders. The back should be straight, not swayed. The neck should be sleek. Legs need to be long and slim. (Think of a ballet dancer.) The hind legs are higher than the front legs. The paws should be oval. There should be five toes in the front and four toes on the rear paws. The tail should be long and whiplike, thin at the base, and tapered to a fine point.

The coat on an Oriental Shorthair should be short and close-lying. The coat pattern may be solid, shaded, smoke, particolor, bicolor, pointed, or

An Oriental is long, muscular, surprisingly heavy, and has a tubular shape.

tabby. Tabbies may be mackerel, spotted, ticked, or classic. The basic coat color will be white, red, cream, ebony, blue, chestnut, lavender, and cinnamon or fawn. Pointed Orientals may be any of the nine colors and may be tabby, particolor, or bicolor. In show rings throughout the world, they are usually shown as Siamese, with the same standard used for both breeds. They were created to be equal, and most breeders of Pointed Orientals want them to remain equal.

ORIENTAL COLORS
Solid Color Class

This is the basic Oriental, with the same color from the tip of his tail to the tips of his ears and all the way to his toes.

Pointed Class

Pointed Orientals may come in any of the accepted colors and their combinations. They may be shown in ACFA as Pointed Orientals, TICA as Siamese, and most of the other associations as Siamese. Many of them have been shown in CFA from 1984 until the present as Colorpoint Shorthairs and have earned regional and breed titles.

Tabby Color Class

An Oriental with one of the basic colors (except white) plus a tabby pattern is a tabby. Add the silver modifier (when the fur has silver roots) and the cat will be a Blue Silver Tabby, Red Silver Tabby, etc.

The head of an Oriental should be wedge-shaped with a long, straight profile.

Shaded Color Class

With more silver in the fur so that color is restricted to just the tips of the hair, the cat is one of these colors: Blue Silver, Chestnut Silver, etc.

Smoke Color Class

Smoke cats are one of the basic Oriental colors (except white) but with a touch of silver. You should not be able to tell that the cat is silver until she moves or you brush her hair back.

Bicolor Color Class

Bicolor cats should have the basic colors for any color of Oriental Solids, Tabbies, Particolors, Shadeds, and Smokes, *plus* various degrees of white.

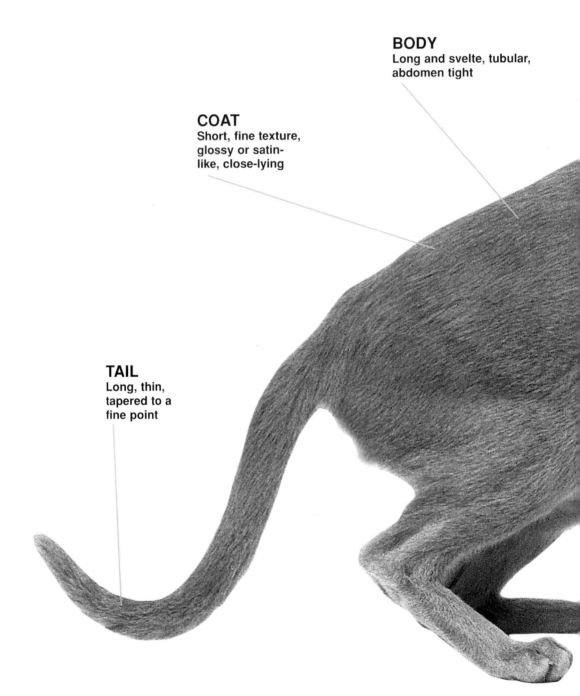

BODY
Long and svelte, tubular, abdomen tight

COAT
Short, fine texture, glossy or satin-like, close-lying

TAIL
Long, thin, tapered to a fine point

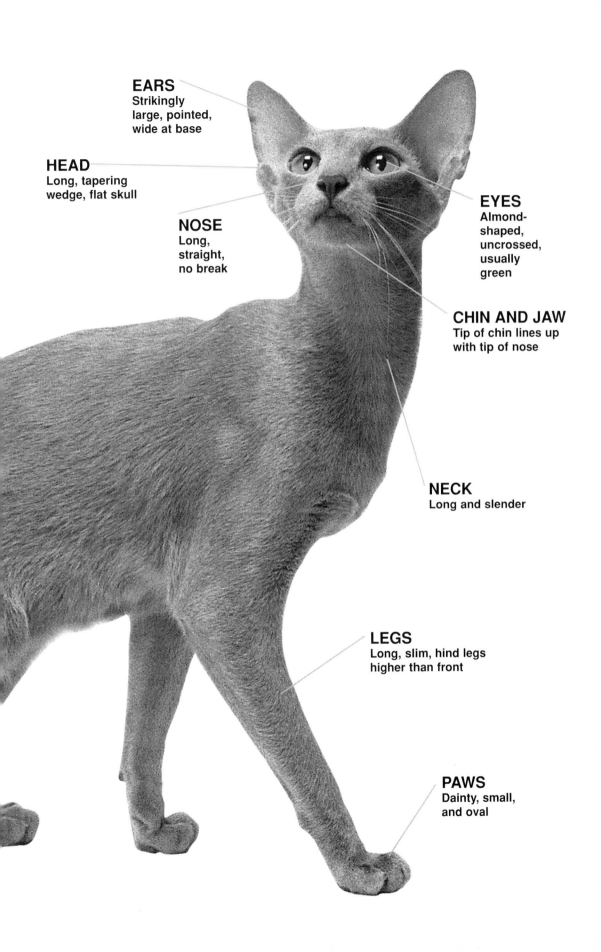

EARS
Strikingly
large, pointed,
wide at base

HEAD
Long, tapering
wedge, flat skull

NOSE
Long,
straight,
no break

EYES
Almond-
shaped,
uncrossed,
usually
green

CHIN AND JAW
Tip of chin lines up
with tip of nose

NECK
Long and slender

LEGS
Long, slim, hind legs
higher than front

PAWS
Dainty, small,
and oval

Particolor Color Class

These cats have a basic coat of one of the first colors *plus* patches of the second color.

CFA BREED STANDARD: ORIENTAL

This standard has been reprinted with the permission of the Cat Fanciers' Association. Note that the standard for this breed includes the Oriental Longhair, which was accepted by the CFA in 1995.

Point Score

Head (20)
Long, flat profile 6
Wedge, fine muzzle, size 5
Ears 4
Chin 3
Width between eyes 2

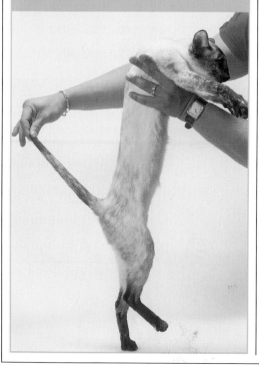

A whiplike tail that is long, thin, and tapered to a fine point is part of the Oriental breed standard.

Eyes (10)
Shape, size, slant,
and placement 10
Body (30)
Structure and size,
including neck 12
Muscle tone 10
Legs and Feet 5
Tail 3
Coat (10)
Color (30)
Coat color (color 10;
pattern 10) 20
Eye color (10)

General

The ideal Oriental is a svelte cat with long, tapering lines, very lithe but muscular. Excellent physical condition. Eyes clear. Strong and lithe, neither bony nor flabby. Not fat. Because of the longer coat the Longhair Division appears to have softer lines and less extreme type than the Shorthair Division.

Head

Long tapering wedge, in good proportion to body. The total wedge starts at the nose and flares out in straight lines to the tips of the ears forming a triangle, with no break at the whiskers. No less than the width of an eye between the eyes. When the whiskers (and face hair for the Longhair Division) are smoothed back, the underlying bone structure is apparent. Allowance must be made for jowls in the stud cat.
Skull—flat. In profile, a long straight line is seen from the top of the head to the tip of the nose. No bulge over eyes. No dip in nose.

Nose—long and straight. A continuation of the forehead with no break.

Muzzle—fine, wedge-shaped.

Chin and Jaw—medium size. Tip of chin lines up with tip of nose in the same vertical plane. Neither receding nor excessively massive.

Ears—strikingly large, pointed, wide at the base, continuing the lines of the wedge.

Eyes—almond shaped, medium size. Neither protruding nor recessed. Slanted towards the nose in harmony with lines of wedge and ears. Uncrossed.

Body

Long and svelte. A distinctive combination of fine bones and firm muscles. Shoulders and hips continue the same sleek lines of tubular body. Hips never wider than shoulders. Abdomen tight. Males may be somewhat larger than females.

Neck—long and slender.

Legs—long and slim. Hind legs higher than front. In good proportion to body.

Paws—dainty, small, and oval. Toes: five in front and four behind.

Tail—long, thin at the base, and tapered to a fine point. Longhair Division: tail hair spreads out like a plume.

Coat (Shorthair Division)—short, fine textured, glossy or satin-like, lying close to body.

Coat (Longhair Division)—medium length, fine, silky, without downy undercoat, lying close to the body, the coat may appear shorter than it is. Hair is longest on the tail.

The Oriental Longhair, accepted by the CFA in 1995, is included in the Oriental standard. It is judged in the Longhair Division.

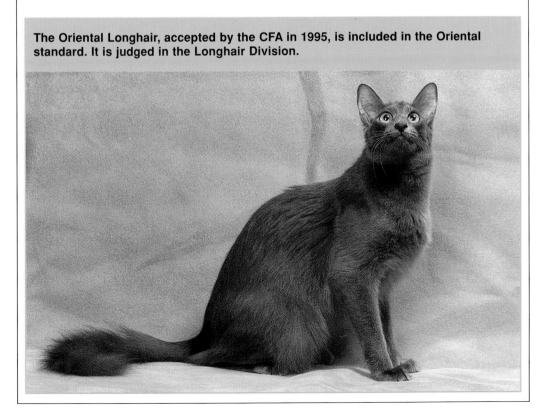

Coat Color

A distinguishing feature of the Oriental is the coat color, whether solid, shaded, smoke, particolor, bicolor or tabby patterned. *Solid—* In the solid color cat, the coat color should be of uniform density and color from the tip to the root of each hair and from the nose to the tail. The full coat color score (20) should be used to assess the quality and the correctness of the color. *Shaded—*The shaded cat has a white undercoat, with a mantle of colored tipping shading down from the sides, face and tail from dark on the ridge to white on the chin, chest underside and under the tail. *Smoke—*Cat in repose appears solid in color. In motion the color is clearly apparent. Extremities are solid in color, and have a narrow band of white at the base of hairs next to the skin which may be seen only when the fur is parted. *Particolor—* A solid* cat with patches of red or softly intermingled areas of red on both body and extremities (presence of several shades of red acceptable; *dilute colors exhibit cream instead of red). *Bicolor—* Bicolors should conform to the established standard for their co-existing pattern, with the addition of white feet, legs, underside, chest and muzzle, including an inverted "V" blaze on the face. *Tabby—*In the tabby patterned cat, the quality of the pattern is an essential part of the cat. The pattern should match the description for the particular pattern and be well defined. The pattern should be viewed while the cat is in a natural standing position. The remaining ten points are allotted to the correctness of the color, it matches the color description. **Eye Color**—green. White Orientals and bicolor Orientals may have blue, green or odd-eyed eye color.

Penalize

Crossed eyes. Palpable and/or visible protrusion of the cartilage at the end of the sternum.

Disqualify

Any evidence of illness or poor health. Weak hind legs. Mouth breathing due to nasal obstruction or poor occlusion. Emaciation. Visible kink in tail. Miniaturization. Lockets and buttons. Incorrect number of toes. Longhair Division: definite double coat (i.e. downy undercoat).

Oriental Colors

Solid Color Class—BLUE: blue, one level tone from nose to tip of tail. Sound to the roots. *Nose leather and paw pads:* blue. **CHESTNUT:** rich chestnut brown, sound throughout. Whiskers and *Nose leather:* same color as coat. *Paw pads:* cinnamon. **CINNAMON:** a light reddish brown, distinctly warmer and lighter than chestnut, sound and even throughout. Whiskers same color as coat. *Nose leather and paw pads:* tan to pinkish beige. **CREAM:** one level shade of buff cream, without markings. Sound to the roots. Lighter shades preferred. *Nose leather and paw pads:* pink. **EBONY:** dense coal black, sound from roots to tip of fur. Free from any tinge of rust on tips or smoke undercoat. *Nose leather:* black. *Paw pads:* black or brown. **FAWN:** a light lavender with pale cocoa overtones, sound and even throughout. *Nose leather and paw pads:* a light shade of dusty rose pink (no blue or lavender tones). Whiskers same color as coat. **LAVENDER:** frosty-grey with a pinkish tone, sound and even throughout. *Nose leather and paw pads:* lavender-pink. **RED:** deep, rich, clear, brilliant red; without shading, markings, or ticking. Lips and chin the same color as coat. *Nose leather and paw pads:* flesh or coral pink. **WHITE:** pure, glistening white. *Nose leather and paw pads:* pink. **Shaded Color Class—BLUE SILVER:** undercoat white with a mantle of blue tipping shading down from sides, face and tail from dark on the ridge to white on the chin, chest, underside and under the tail. Legs to be the same tone as the face. Rims of eyes, lips and nose outlined with blue. *Nose leather:* old rose. *Paw pads:* blue. **CHESTNUT SILVER:** undercoat white with a mantle of chestnut tipping shading down from sides, face and tail from dark on the ridge to white on the chin, chest, underside and under the tail. Legs to be the same tone as the face. Rims of eyes, lips and nose outlined with chestnut. *Nose leather:* pink. Paw pads: coral pink. **CINNAMON SILVER:** undercoat white with a mantle of cinnamon tipping shading down from sides, face and tail from dark on the ridge to white on the chin, chest, underside and under the tail. Legs to be the same tone

as the face. Rims of eyes, lips and nose outlined with cinnamon. *Nose leather:* pink. *Paw pads:* coral pink. **CREAM SILVER (Dilute Cameo):** undercoat white with a mantle of cream tipping shading down from sides, face and tail from dark on the ridge to white on the chin, chest, underside and under the tail. Legs to be the same tone as the face. *Nose leather, rims of eyes and paw pads:* pink. **EBONY SILVER:** undercoat white with a mantle of black tipping shading down from sides, face and tail from dark on the ridge to white on the chin, chest, underside and under the tail. Legs to be the same tone as the face. Rims of eyes, lips and nose outlined with black. *Nose leather:* brick red. *Paw pads:* black. **FAWN SILVER:** undercoat white with a mantle of fawn tipping shading down from sides, face and tail from dark on the ridge to white on the chin, chest, underside and under the tail. Legs to be the same tone as the face. Rims of eyes, lips and nose outlined with fawn. *Nose leather:* pink. *Paw pads:* pink. **LAVENDER SILVER:** undercoat white with a mantle of lavender tipping shading down from sides, face and tail from dark on the ridge to white on the chin, chest, underside and under the tail. Legs to be the same tone as the face. Rims of eyes, lips and nose outlined with lavender. *Nose leather:* lavender pink. *Paw pads:* lavender pink. **PARTICOLOR SILVER:** undercoat white with a mantle of black, blue*, chestnut, cinnamon, fawn* or lavender* tipping with patches of red or softly intermingled areas of red on both body and extremities (presence of several shades of red acceptable; *dilute colors exhibit cream instead of red), shading down from sides, face and tail from dark on the ridge to white on the chin, chest, underside and under the tail. *Nose leather:* may be mottled with pink. *Paw pads:* may be mottled with pink. **RED SILVER (Cameo):** undercoat white with a mantle of red tipping shading down from sides, face and tail from dark on the ridge to white on the chin, chest, underside and under the tail. Legs to be the same tone as the face. *Nose leather, rims of eyes and paw pads:* rose. **Smoke Color Class—BLUE SMOKE:** white undercoat, deeply tipped with blue. Cat in repose appears blue. In motion the white undercoat is clearly apparent. Points and mask blue with narrow band of white at base of hairs next to skin which may be seen only when fur is parted. *Nose leather and paw pads:* blue. **RED SMOKE (Cameo Smoke):** white undercoat, deeply tipped with red. Cat in repose appears red. In motion the white undercoat is clearly apparent. Points and mask red with narrow band of white at base of hairs next to skin which may be seen only when fur is parted. *Nose leather, rims of eyes and paw pads:* rose. **CHESTNUT SMOKE:** white undercoat, deeply tipped with chestnut brown. Cat in repose appears chestnut brown. In motion the white undercoat is

clearly apparent. Points and mask chestnut brown with narrow band of white at base of hairs next to skin which may be seen only when fur is parted. *Nose leather and paw pads:* lavender-pink. **CINNAMON SMOKE:** white undercoat, deeply tipped with cinnamon. Cat in repose appears cinnamon. In motion the white undercoat is clearly apparent. Points and mask cinnamon with narrow band of white at base of hairs which may be seen only when fur is parted. *Nose leather:* cinnamon. *Paw pads:* coral. **CREAM SMOKE (Dilute Cameo Smoke):** white undercoat deeply tipped with cream. Cat in repose appears cream. In motion the white undercoat is clearly apparent. Points and mask cream with narrow base of white at base of hairs next to skin which may be seen only when the fur is parted. *Nose leather, rims of eyes, and paw pads:* pink. **EBONY SMOKE:** white undercoat, deeply tipped with black. Cat in repose appears black. In motion the white undercoat is clearly apparent. Points and mask black with narrow band of white at base of hairs next to skin which may be seen only when fur is parted. *Nose leather and paw pads:* black. **FAWN SMOKE:** white undercoat, deeply tipped with fawn. Cat in repose appears fawn. In motion the white undercoat is clearly apparent. Points and mask fawn with narrow band of white at base of hairs which may be seen only when fur is parted. *Nose leather:* fawn. *Paw pads:* pink. **LAVENDER SMOKE:** white undercoat, deeply tipped with lavender. Cat in repose appears lavender. In motion the white undercoat is clearly apparent. Points and mask lavender with narrow band of white at base of hairs next to skin which may be seen only when fur is parted. *Nose leather and paw pads:* lavender-pink.

PARTICOLOR SMOKE: white undercoat deeply tipped with black, blue*, chestnut, cinnamon, fawn* or lavender* tipping with patches of red or softly intermingled areas of red on both body and extremities (presence of several shades of red acceptable; *dilute colors exhibit cream instead of red), as in the pattern of the Particolor. Cat in repose appears Particolor. In motion, the white undercoat is clearly apparent. Face and ears have Particolor pattern with a narrow band of white at the base of the hairs next to the skin, which may be seen only when the fur is parted. *Nose leather and paw pads:* may be mottled with pink.

Tabby Color Class—CLASSIC TABBY PATTERN: markings dense, clearly defined, and broad. Legs evenly barred with bracelets coming up to meet the body markings. Tail evenly ringed. Several unbroken necklaces on neck and upper chest, the more the better. Frown marks on forehead form an intricate letter "M." Unbroken line runs back from outer corner of eye. Swirls on cheeks. Vertical lines over back of head extend to shoulder markings which are in the shape of a butterfly with both upper and lower wings distinctly outlined and marked with dots inside outline. Back markings consist of a vertical line down the spine from butterfly to tail with a vertical stripe paralleling it on each side, the three stripes well separated by stripes of the ground color. Large solid blotch on each side to be encircled by one or more unbroken rings. Side markings should be the same on both sides. Double vertical rows of buttons on chest and stomach. **MACKEREL TABBY PATTERN:** markings dense, clearly defined, and all narrow pencillings. Legs evenly barred with narrow bracelets coming up to meet the body markings. Tail barred. Necklaces on neck and chest distinct, like so many chains. Head barred with an "M" on the forehead. Unbroken lines running back from the eyes. Lines running down the head to meet the shoulders. Spine lines run together to form a narrow saddle. Narrow pencillings run around body. **SPOTTED TABBY PATTERN:** markings on the body to be spotted. May vary in size and shape with preference given to round, evenly distributed spots. Spots should not run together in a broken Mackerel pattern. A dorsal stripe runs the length of the body to the tip of the tail. The stripe is ideally composed of spots. The markings on the face and forehead shall be typically tabby markings. Underside of the body to have "vest buttons." Legs and tail are barred. **TICKED TABBY PATTERN:** body hairs to be ticked with various shades of marking color and ground color. Body when viewed from top to be free from noticeable spots, stripes, or blotches, except for darker dorsal shading. Lighter underside may show tabby markings. Face, legs, and tail must show distinct tabby striping. Cat must have at least one distinct necklace. **PATCHED TABBY PATTERN:** a patched tabby is an established Classic, Mackerel, Spotted or Ticked Tabby in blue*, chestnut, cinnamon, ebony, fawn* or lavender*, or any of these colors in silver, with patches of red or softly intermingled areas of red on both body and extremities (presence of several shades of red acceptable; *dilute colors exhibit cream instead of red). *Nose leather and paw pads:* same as non-patched tabbies, may be mottled with pink. **BLUE SILVER TABBY:** ground color, including lips and chin, pale, clear bluish silver. Markings sound blue. *Nose leather:* blue or old rose trimmed with blue. *Paw pads:* blue. **BLUE TABBY:** ground color, including lips and chin, pale bluish ivory. Markings a very deep blue affording a good contrast with ground color. Warm fawn overtones or patina over the whole. *Nose leather:* blue, or old rose trimmed with blue. *Paw pads:* bluish rose. **RED SILVER TABBY (Cameo Tabby):** ground color off-white. Markings red. *Nose leather and paw pads:* rose. **CREAM SILVER TABBY (Dilute Cameo Tabby):** ground color off-white. Markings cream. *Nose leather and paw pads:* pink. **CINNAMON SILVER TABBY:** ground color, including lips and chin, pale glistening silver. Markings dense cinnamon.

Nose leather: cinnamon, or pink rimmed with cinnamon. *Paw pads:* coral pink. **CINNAMON TABBY:** ground color, including lips and chin, a pale warm honey, markings a dense cinnamon, affording a good contrast with ground color. *Nose leather:* cinnamon or coral rimmed with cinnamon. *Paw pads:* cinnamon. **CHESTNUT SILVER TABBY:** ground color, including lips and chin, a snowy silver. Markings rich chestnut. *Nose leather:* chestnut, or pink rimmed with chestnut. *Paw pads:* coral pink. **CHESTNUT TABBY:** ground color warm fawn. Markings are rich chestnut. *Nose leather:* chestnut, or pink rimmed with chestnut. *Paw pads:* cinnamon. **CREAM TABBY:** ground color, including lips and chin, very pale cream. Markings of buff or cream sufficiently darker than the ground color to afford good contrast but remaining within the dilute color range. *Nose leather and paw pads:* pink. **EBONY TABBY:** ground color brilliant coppery brown. Markings dense black. Lips and chin the same shade as the rings around the eyes. Back of leg black from paw to heel. *Nose leather:* black, or brick red rimmed with black. *Paw pads:* black or brown. **FAWN TABBY:** ground color, including lips and chin, pale ivory. Markings dense fawn, affording good contrast with ground color. *Nose leather and paw pads:* pale fawn. **FAWN SILVER TABBY:** ground color, including lips and chin, pale glistening silver. Markings dense fawn. *Nose leather:* fawn, or pink rimmed with fawn. *Paw pads:*

pink. **LAVENDER SILVER TABBY:** ground color, including lips and chin, a cold clear silver. Markings sound lavender. *Nose leather:* lavender, or pink rimmed with lavender. *Paw pads:* lavender-pink. **LAVENDER TABBY:** ground color is pale lavender. Markings are rich lavender affording a good contrast with the ground color. *Nose leather:* lavender, or pink rimmed with lavender. *Paw pads:* lavender-pink. **RED TABBY:** ground color red. Markings deep, rich red. Lips and chin red. *Nose leather and paw pads:* flesh or coral pink.

EBONY SILVER TABBY: ground color, including lips and chin, pale clear silver. Markings dense black. *Nose leather:* black, or brick red rimmed with black. *Paw pads:* black.

Bicolor Color Class—All cats conform to the established colors and patterns for Particolors, Shadeds, Smokes, Solids and Tabbies with the addition of white. Calicos should be a white cat with unbrindled patches of blue*, chestnut, cinnamon, ebony, lavender* or fawn* with patches of red or softly intermingled areas of red (presence of several shades of red acceptable; *dilute colors exhibit cream instead of red). Van Calico color should be confined to the extremities, except that one or two small patches on the body are allowable. As a preferred minimum, all Bicolors should have white feet, legs, underside, chest and muzzle. Less than this minimum should be penalized proportionally. Nose leather and

Tortoiseshell Orientals like this one, GRC, GRP Katwildo Tuff-E-Nuff, are classified as particolor cats.

paw pads conform to the established standards.

Particolor Color Class—BLUE CREAM: blue mottled or patched with cream. **CINNAMON TORTOISESHELL:** cinnamon with patches of red or softly intermingled areas of red on both body and extremities (presence of several shades of red acceptable). **CHESTNUT TORTOISESHELL:** chestnut brown with patches of red or softly intermingled areas of red on both body and extremities (presence of several shades of red acceptable). **FAWN-CREAM:** fawn mottled or patched with cream. **LAVENDER-CREAM:** lavender mottled or patched with cream. **EBONY TORTOISESHELL:** black with patches of red or softly intermingled areas of red on both body and extremities (presence of several shades of red acceptable).

LOCATING AN ORIENTAL SHORTHAIR

There are many places to find Oriental kittens, because they are shown in every association around the world. Some people want to see them first and some want to research them first—it's your choice. Most Oriental breeders do not encourage you to make an impulsive purchase, so you are safe either way.

AT A SHOW

A cat show is a wonderful opportunity to view several Orientals at once. Usually, there will be several colors and patterns for you to see, different breeders and exhibitors to talk to, and kittens for sale. You can watch the kitten class, the championship class, and the premiership (altered) class. Each ring is a show of its own with different judges, and each judge will have his/her own top cats.

Walk around and see the cats in their cages. Chances are that owners of Orientals will have one of their cats in their arms or on their shoulders or playing with a toy. Breeders may talk to you about kittens for sale that are at the show hall. Sometimes, they will tell you about a litter that is at home because the kittens are too young to go to a new home. They may have photos of past or present kittens or cats or other information to share with you.

Don't be too surprised if you find yourself being asked many questions by the breeder. They will want to know *your* past cat experiences. Do you have any cats now? How old are they? What breed? Are they neutered and spayed? Are they declawed? Do they stay indoors 100 percent of the time? Who takes care of your cats when you go on vacation? They will want to know all about the cats that you have had in the past. Oriental breeders want their kittens to be placed in a permanent, well-adjusted, loving home for life.

If you do not have any cats at home, most breeders will suggest that you acquire two cats instead of one. If you do not want to purchase two kittens, there is often a retired show or breeding cat that the kitten has a good

Attending a cat show is a wonderful opportunity to view several Orientals in one place. There will be lots of different colors and patterns to see, breeders and exhibitors to talk to, and kittens for sale.

relationship with that will be also looking for a home. These cats are often young cats that just did not enjoy shows. They may have already earned their grand champion title or had to be spayed, or the breeder may need to give them up for a variety of other reasons. They deserve loving owners who can give them more attention than the breeder can.

If you do purchase a kitten or adult at a show, there are always vendors there who will sell you a cat carrier and all of the supplies that you will need for your new Oriental. You can bring a carrier in the back seat of your car just in case you find the perfect kitten.

Schedules of cat shows may be found in some of the cat magazines. These are sometimes available at your local library. There are also listings in the cat association magazines, which you probably will not have subscribed to unless you are already a breeder or exhibitor. The easiest place to find these cat show schedules is on the Internet. Each cat association has its own Web site and devotes space to its show schedule. On some sites, there is a spectator list and an exhibitor section. You can also write or call the association directly and ask when there will be a show in your area.

FINDING A BREEDER

Finding breeders of Oriental cats is even easier than finding a show to attend. When you write or call a cat association, ask them for a list of breeders in a specific area. Some of the

If you do not have any cats at home, most breeders will suggest that you acquire two Orientals instead of one. One option is to provide a home for an adult, retired show or breeding cat.

associations have breeder listings on their Web sites.

There are several Internet sites that have breeder listings, and if you do a search, you will find hundreds of breeders around the world. Write or call them. If they do not have kittens, ask them if they know of any in the color or pattern that you are looking for. Most breeders will help you find the right kitten even if it is not one of their kittens.

You can also locate breeders through e-mail. There is an e-mail list for Oriental Shorthair enthusiasts that has more than 100 members. (Subscription instructions for this and other e-mail lists are listed later in this book.) It is a good place to ask questions, observe, and learn about all aspects of the breed. It is not affiliated with any one association, and members are from all over the world. The members of the list are always congratulating someone on a good show or a beautiful new litter.

HOW TO CHOOSE A KITTEN

Choosing a kitten is fun, but you should never buy one on impulse. A kitten should be thought of as a way of life. You may be living with this cat for 20 years. Where do you see yourself in 10 or 15 years? If you are thinking of retiring and traveling a lot, for example, what will the kitten do?

An Oriental kitten is a bouncing bundle of energy, only occasionally resting or sleeping. All corners of your home will be explored, including the tops of bookcases, the refrigerator, and your china cabinet. Accidents can and will occur. If your collectibles

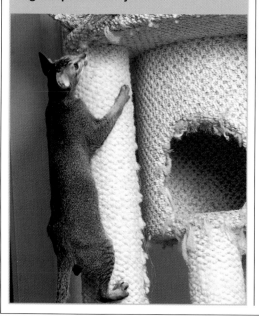

An Oriental kitten is a bouncing bundle of energy, only occasionally resting or sleeping. Is an energetic, outgoing cat perfect for you?

break, it is your fault because you have been warned about the curiosity of your Oriental Shorthair. Please do not blame your cat for being herself.

If an energetic, outgoing cat would be the perfect addition to your household, ask yourself the following questions:

Do you want a cat for pet, breed, or show? Do you have a color preference? Do you prefer a certain pattern?

If you are thinking of showing your cat, do you prefer one cat association to another? Which has more shows in your area? Which association shares your beliefs about registering, showing, and acceptance of colors?

E-mail and call breeders. Ask many questions. Show them how interested you are in having one of their kittens. In turn, they will ask you many questions. It is an interview process for both of you, and the match is not always correct. You must find a breeder that you enjoy working with.

If you are looking for a silver tabby female kitten and you only find breeders who have males or cats that are non-silver or non-tabby, ask for a referral. Most breeders will know someone who may have just what you are looking for. On the other hand, if you have already met the breeder you would like to work with, ask them if they have a waiting list for kittens.

You should visit your kitten to make sure that this is the little guy or girl you would choose to live with for the next 20 years. If you are working with a breeder from a distance, ask for a videotape of the kitten, the parents, older siblings, and the surroundings. This will give you a much more accurate impression than a snapshot. Your kitten or cat should appear healthy and happy, with bright eyes and shiny fur. Never buy a kitten that appears to be sick for any reason.

Most breeders will not sell you a kitten until she is 16 weeks old. Some will neuter or spay young kittens before they leave the house. Some will add a neuter/spay contract as a condition of the sale. Many will withhold registration papers until they receive proof of spaying or neutering. Most will give you a pedigree and probably a photocopy of the registration. You should also receive a vaccination record and a health record at the time of purchase, which you will want to share with your vet.

Most breeders ask that you contact them once a year to tell them how their little baby is growing up. Many will contact you through mail, phone, e-mail, newsletter, or at shows. It is important that you do not lose contact. If your cat becomes ill, the breeder may be able to offer advice. If a relative of your cat develops a disease, it may be important that the breeder warn you of signs and symptoms.

It is normal for there to be a contract between the breeder

If at all possible, visit the breeder to make sure your chosen kitten is the right little guy or girl for you.

and kitten buyer. It should spell out what each party expects of the other. For example, a breeder will ask that you take good care of your cat, take her to the vet, give her vaccinations, keep her indoors only, trim her nails once a week and never declaw her, send you a photo once a year, and may have other conditions such as spaying or neutering. You are asking for a kitten that is healthy and free of known disease, has registration papers and a pedigree, is sociable, and is socially ready to go to his new home. A sample kitten sale contract from our cattery will give you a good idea of a typical agreement:

A healthy Oriental kitten or cat should be active and happy, with shiny eyes and fur.

KITTEN SALE CONTRACT (SAMPLE)

Algebra Cattery
Victor, Lynn, and Rachel Miller
(name, address, and phone number)

Breed: Oriental Shorthair, Registered with CFA
Color: Ebony Smoke
Sex: male
Registered Name: Algebra's Lone Ranger
Call Name: Ranger
Price $
Sellers:
Buyers:
(name, address, and phone number)
Date of sale: _____

Buyers' Signatures _____

Sellers' Signatures _____

Sale Conditions:
- Cat or kitten will not be declawed.
- Cat or kitten will not be allowed outdoors.
- Cat or kitten will be neutered or spayed prior to its first birthday.
- Cat or kitten will not be used or resold as breeding "stock."
- Cat or kitten will not be sold to any lab for animal testing.
- Cat or kitten will see a licensed veterinarian at least once a year for life.
- Cat or kitten will receive inoculations on an annual basis or as suggested by veterinarian.
- Cat or kitten will NOT receive any inoculation claiming to be effective against FeLV or FIP.
- Algebra Cattery likes to keep in touch with the owners through the years. It is also good to know where

Sample Contract, cont.

offspring are in case any hereditary condition is found.

- Buyer will notify Algebra Cattery if buyer cannot keep cat for any reason.
- Buyer will notify Algebra Cattery of any address changes.
- Buyer will send a photo of the cat and note once a year.
- Buyer will notify Algebra Cattery if cat is shown and any awards are received.
- Cattery is registered with CFA, TICA, and CFF. All of our cats are CFA-registered. Most of our cats are TICA-registered. Your cat is "showable" and may be shown.
- We recommend that any pointed Oriental be shown in TICA, because they are recognized as Siamese.

- Pedigree is included, and if you go to a cat show, it is fun to find relatives.
- Registration papers will be sent after kitten is neutered. You have copies now. Please complete your registration papers as soon as you receive them. If you are undecided about a name, please know that for a small fee, it can always be changed. If you wait, you may lose the papers and they are not easy to have duplicated. We hope to speak with you several times over the next few weeks. Please feel free to call us with questions.
- Siamese and Oriental kittens and cats are highly active. They will run, jump, and climb. Most reach the ceiling at least once in their first year. They will go through any open

Most Oriental kittens will reach the ceiling at least once in their first year. This breed loves to climb.

Sample Contract, cont.

door out of curiosity—outside, closet, pantry, etc. Beware of plants—make sure that they are not poisonous and that the cats do not eat them.

• Water should be available at all times—a stainless steel bowl is best because some cats develop acne on their chin from plastic dishes. Crockery may contain lead, and no breakable container should be used.

• Dry food may be free-fed. Premium brands are recommended and may be purchased in most pet stores.

• Feeding canned food morning and evening is recommended. Premium brands are preferred.

• A kitten should eat four times a day, with one of those meals being just before you go to sleep.

One essential supply for every cat-owning household is a litter box. Unlike with puppies, no housetraining will be required for your new Oriental kitten.

A responsible breeder will expect you to keep your cat's nails trimmed and never declaw her.

• You need a litter box, or boxes if you have more than one floor. Sometimes kittens play hard and forget or need to find the box in a hurry. One box for every two cats is a rule of thumb. Your kitten is used to regular clay litter with a plastic liner, changed once a day. We do not recommend clumping litter, because it is a perfect breeding ground for bacteria and is very dangerous if the cat eats it while cleaning himself or herself.

• Claws should be clipped once a week as a rule, but if the cat is living with dogs, he or she may need the claws for defense. A brief brushing

Sample Contract, cont.

with a rubber brush is good for the cat too. A bath is not necessary for your short-haired cat. We use self-rinsing shampoo when necessary.

• Toilet seats should be down at all times to prevent your cat from drowning.

• Food disposal should be covered.

• Windows should be screened.

• A carrier should always be used to carry the cat outdoors. We place a seat belt around the carrier in the car. It is safer than carrying the cat in your arms and is much safer in the car.

• Introduce other animals slowly. Keep the new kitten in your bedroom so that it becomes used to you first, and introduce other animals one at a time. It may take two weeks or more for your animals to accept the kitten. Do not leave them all alone together until you are sure that there will be no problems.

A carrier is necessary when transporting your Oriental cat outdoors. It will keep the cat calm and is much safer in the car.

Introduce other animals slowly to your new cat or kitten. Isolate the new arrival at first and supervise all interactions for several weeks. Here, ebony ticked tabby kitten Patipause Majimece and seal lynx-point GC Patipause Lisap renew their acquaintance.

FEEDING

Healthy Orientals do not have different diet needs than other cats. Just like all cats, they are carnivores and require protein, minerals, carbohydrates, vitamins, and water. We are very lucky that we have such a large variety of commercial foods to choose from.

KITTENS

Kittens need more protein than adults and they need to be fed more often. Most good brands of cat food have special kitten formulas. From the time that they begin to eat solid foods at about 5 weeks of age until the age of 16 weeks, they should be fed 4 meals a day. At 16 weeks, they will usually do fine with 3 meals a day.

Depending on how they look and act and how much dry food they consume, you will probably want to reevaluate their diets at six and nine months of age. Switching to adult cat food at one year of age is recommended.

FREE OR CONTROLLED FEEDINGS?

This will depend on your household and your cats. With one cat or kitten, it is easy to fill a bowl with dry food and allow your

Whether to provide free or controlled feedings depends on the household and the cats in question. Just like this cinnamon Oriental Shorthair, most cats like to munch all day, but many cats eat too much if food is always available.

Oriental Shorthairs like GC, GP Algebra's Blue Margarita of Kattalyst are bred to be sleek and in show condition all of the time. Show cats that have trouble keeping their weight down should only be given controlled feedings.

regular food to those that can have it in the evening.

Some Orientals will not eat canned food and like to munch all day, but many cats eat too much if the food is always available. Some vets do not encourage free-feeding because it is unlike the natural state of the cat in the wild. Orientals were not bred to live in the wild, but it is still advisable to remove canned food 30 minutes after it is served.

Orientals are bred to be sleek and in show condition all of the time. Whether they are free-fed or not, with a few minutes of grooming, most should be ready for the show bench at any time. Some Orientals are not as lucky and need to have controlled

cat access to it 24 hours a day. This is especially true if you will be out of the house for more than eight hours at a time. Multiple-cat households often do this too.

However, in a multi-cat house, there may be cats on special diets for diseases, allergies, or breeding purposes, and free-feeding will not be an acceptable method. For some diseases or for breeding, extra calories may be required, so the affected cats can free-feed on the regular food during the day and be fed extra kitten food in the evening. If you have a cat with renal or heart disease or allergies, sometimes it is easier to feed all the cats the special diet (with your vet's OK) and give the

Many owners of Orientals cook for their cats or treat them to occasional table scraps. Leftover turkey is always a favorite.

feedings while they are being shown to keep their weight down.

SPECIAL HEALTH DIET

There are special foods for cats with cardiac, renal, bladder, allergy, and intestinal problems, as well as for other needs. These foods are sold by prescription only, usually through your vet. Sometimes it may take a while to get your cat to enjoy these foods, but other times, they like them immediately.

COOKING FOR YOUR CAT

Many owners of Orientals cook for their cats. Beef and chicken are the most popular foods, but scallops, lamb, veal, vegetables, rice, and potatoes are also common. There are several books available on feline nutrition that include recipes.

Your Oriental will also like to eat leftover chicken, turkey, salmon, and tuna. (Please be very careful with the bones.) Some will eat cheese, eggs, spaghetti, rice, potatoes, vegetables, and fruit. A few will eat cookies, muffins, potato chips, and other foods that they really do not need. Feed your cats treats like these only very occasionally.

THE PREGNANT CAT

A pregnant cat, or queen, will require more protein and more food while she is pregnant and even more while she is nursing her babies. Many breeders give the queen kitten food several times a day in either the canned

Some human foods aren't good for cats. However, that doesn't stop Premier Algebra's P Squared of Kattalyst, who thinks cream-cheese frosting is yummy.

The pregnant or nursing queen needs extra protein and more food to support her kittens and maintain her own health. Many breeders feed their mother cats kitten food several times a day.

cats eat the paper plates, so they have to find an alternative.

WATER

Orientals need to have fresh water available to them at all times. Occasionally, tap water has the smell or taste of chemicals, and a cat will refuse to drink it. The easiest way to solve this dilemma is to use bottled or filtered water. This is advisable anyway to prevent illnesses such as giardia. Water bowls should be washed daily, not just refilled. Bacteria can multiply in a dirty dish.

THE SENIOR CAT

Your special friend has different needs when she is a

or dry version. Some give additional vitamins and minerals.

FOOD DISHES

Many Orientals tend to get chin acne. Plastic food dishes and allergies to food cause this. I always recommend stainless steel bowls for water. They are available in many different sizes, are inexpensive and unbreakable, can go into the dishwasher, and last for years. Dry food dishes should be washed when empty. An extra set to use while the other is in the dishwasher is advisable.

Orientals seem to like eating canned food on flat dishes as opposed to cups or bowls. I prefer paper plates for canned food, but any flat plate will work. Some people have told me that their

Champion Algebra's Yahoo isn't too fussy about what this bowl is made out of, but many cats are allergic to plastic food and water dishes. Ceramic and stainless steel bowls are better choices.

Fresh water must be available to your cats at all times. Using bottled or filtered water may help prevent illnesses such as giardia.

senior citizen than when she was a kitten or young cat. She is not as active and does not need as much protein. Her intestinal system may need a boost with added fiber. She may not have as many teeth as she once did and may require smaller pieces of food. Most of the major premium brand cat foods have special senior cat food formulas. Some vets recommend starting the switch at age 8, while others say 10 or even 12 years old.

WHEN A CAT REFUSES TO EAT

Your cat needs food and water to live. If your cat does not want to eat, something is wrong and she needs veterinary attention. There are supplements in cans and tubes that your vet can give you. Cats usually like them, but you can also mix them with water and feed them with a feeding syringe at home. Your cat can become dehydrated very quickly without eating and drinking and may need the vet to give her fluids under the skin (subcutaneous or "sub-q"). Most vets prefer that a cat that is not feeling well be at home where she can be more comfortable. Home nursing care works in most cases, and your vet can teach you to perform some of the procedures yourself.

FOOD STORAGE

All commercial cat food has a shelf life. If it is dry food, when the bag is opened, it is advisable to pour it into an airtight container. There are many large containers available for purchase in catalogs, pet stores, and department stores. Some pet owners store dry food in the refrigerator or freezer.

Canned food comes in different sizes. If possible, buy the right size for one meal. Cats do not like leftover cat food even when it's reheated to room temperature in the microwave. If you do reheat, please check the temperature, just as you would do for a baby, before feeding the food to your cat. A burnt tongue hurts! If you must save canned food, it should be transferred to a storage container. Storing food in the open can allows the metals and oxygen to mix with the food.

HOUSEHOLD SAFETY

We must protect our pets from us. There are dangerous things in our homes. If you don't believe it, crawl around the floor and see things through your cat's eyes. New parents childproof their home for the new infant or toddler, and living with an Oriental is like living with a toddler. Dangerous objects must be removed, never let into the home, or handled with extreme care. The following is not a complete list of dangers, but indicates some of the most common problems.

MEDICATIONS

All of your medications must be in a closed cabinet. Cats are curious. They will taste your pills, bite into a tube, or walk off with a whole vial of pills to hear this new "cat toy" make noise. Over-the-counter medications such as acetaminophen and aspirin are poisonous, and even one tablet has the potential to kill a cat.

ELECTRICAL OUTLETS

Electricity is a wonderful invention, but it can be deadly to animals. Kittens chew on cords. This can be remedied by putting cords behind furniture, covering them with cord covers, using a taste deterrent containing bitter apple or hot pepper, and just being aware of this danger. Adult cats may spray urine into outlets, which has caused fires. Use the outlet covers that are available in any major store where child safety devices are sold. There are many types available depending on how you use the outlet.

HEIGHTS

Needless to say, windows should have heavy-duty screens on them so that your cat does

Oriental kittens Blue Chip and Calypso may seem at home on the range, but it's important to cat-proof your house to keep curious kitties out of dangerous situations like this.

No matter where you place household plants, your Oriental Shorthair will seek them out. Because so many plants are poisonous, it's probably better not to have them around.

not fall out. If you have lofts, staircases, or ledges, caution is needed. Cats learn from their mistakes, but falling just once from a high place could be deadly. Please take these things into consideration when looking for a new home. It will drive your real estate agent up a wall, but you will feel safe. Your Oriental will climb as high as possible. Remember this when setting up your furniture. Have you created levels and access to the top of your eight-foot-high bookcase?

FURNITURE

Recliners, sofa beds, and rocking chairs can be extremely dangerous to your curious Oriental cat. Your cat may get stuck in chair rungs that are too close together. If you are planning to breed, you should think about tiny kittens when purchasing furniture, installing wrought iron, or changing your staircase design.

Wicker furniture or baskets may be eaten and can be sharp. If your cat's nails are too long, they could get caught in fabric of a chair and she could injure her paw or nail in the struggle to get loose.

DOORS

Doors should only be opened with caution. You may have to do the "cat dance"—a wiggle of the hips as you shut the door quickly, foot extended to block the cat—to go inside and outside without your cat following you. Your Oriental may be one of the climbers that likes to perch on top of an open door. She can get down, but isn't it more fun for her to meow and beg you to climb on a chair to rescue her? Kittens will play behind and around doors, and it is not unusual for one to get caught in the door as it moves. Many owners prop their inside doors open to prevent these injuries to paws, tails, and heads. If you have children in the house, they should be responsible enough to be careful about the cat, not let her outside when their friend comes to the door, and not let her into rooms that are dangerous for her to be in.

PLANTS

If you want to have cats, it is safest not to have plants. If you must have plants, please put them outside. The few times that we have had plants, I have seen cats lick, chew, and eat them. I've also seen them use the planters instead of the litter box. There are hundreds of poisonous plants. You can see lists on these Web pages:

*www.cfainc.org/articles/
plants.html* or
*www.ansci.cornell.edu/plants/
alphalist.html.*

INSECTICIDES

Insects are a problem for everyone, but insecticides are poisonous. Fleas are more than just a nuisance, because they carry infectious diseases, too. You can treat the pet, the home, or both for fleas. Pets can be bathed and can receive topical or oral medications. It is best to speak with your vet about what to do. The important thing is to follow all directions carefully, because too much flea medicine can really harm your cat. Ant or roach baits would almost be impossible to have with an Oriental, because she would find it wherever you hid it. Cats should never play with poisons, of course. If you must have your house sprayed by an exterminator, put all cats in a closed-off area and do not let them out until the solution is dry. Advise the exterminator that you need pet-friendly services.

MOUSE AND RAT POISONS

If you put out mouse or rat baits, make sure they are in a spot that your pet cannot reach. When we have had problems with mice, we have used simple mousetraps with peanut butter as the bait. We hid the traps under the kitchen sink where the cats had no access to them. (Other times, the cats have found the mice and brought them to us.) Anything strong enough to kill a rat will also kill a cat, so please be very careful.

HOUSEHOLD CHEMICALS

Most household chemicals are harmful or deadly if consumed by a feline. Just as with children, cleaning supplies should be out of the cats' reach. They should be stored in a room or cabinet that your cat cannot access. This may mean keeping your pet out of the room where you store such materials. There are many different kinds of childproof and pet-proof cabinet locks for all kinds of cabinets. The nicest looking ones are the ones that you install with screws into the doors of the cabinets. Easier, but less attractive, are the plastic ones that loop through cabinet handles.

OUTDOOR HAZARDS

Oriental Shorthair cat owners do not allow their cats to go outside. These cats are not raised to know the dangers of the outside world. They are intelligent cats, but not street-smart. Visualize what might happen when your favorite feline encounters cars, coyotes, owls, snakes, or cat-hating human beings—just a few of the dangers of being outdoors. Lawnmowers, sleds, children, bicycles, poisons, falls, buses, and trucks are some more. If you need still more reasons, try parasites, fungi, viruses, and bacteria. *There is no reason at all for your Oriental to be outside!*

GARDENING AND LAWN CARE

It would be a good idea to leave your shoes outside after walking on a treated lawn. If you have a dog that goes outside, please be careful. Gardening and lawn supplies should be kept in the garage, outside, or in a place far away from your cats.

AUTOMOBILE CARE SUPPLIES

Your Oriental does not need to "help" you clean your car, add oil, or change the antifreeze. These are very dangerous products to use around your cat. Many pets like the taste of antifreeze, which is a deadly poison to them. Just in case, there are pet-safe antifreeze products on the market. Please consider buying them.

MISCELLANEOUS

Keep pets away from fresh paint, varnish, or stains until these finishes have dried completely. It's not only safer, but it's less messy—have you ever tried to clean white paw prints off of a dark carpet?

BREAKABLES

Your Oriental needs to investigate everything. If you have a favorite figurine or objet d'art, try to find a safe place for it. Some cat owners have told me that they buy glass-enclosed cabinets for their stuff, while others use "quake gel" and florist glue to keep things safe. To sum it up, with Orientals living with you, being careful is a necessity, not a luxury.

Oriental Shorthair cats should not be allowed outside. These indoor cats and kittens at Y-Not Cattery seem to prefer birds on television to the real thing, anyway.

HEALTH CARE AND GROOMING

Your cat's health is important. From the time you choose that cute kitten until she becomes your geriatric friend, you are in charge of her well-being. You are the one who will have to relate any concerns to the veterinarian. In order to do this, you must know what is normal for your cat. You will notice changes in your cat before anyone else, and you need to be observant in order to relay information about your feline friend.

SIGNS OF ILLNESS

You know how your cat acts normally, and playing more or less than usual, sleeping more or less, or being crankier may be signs of illness.

The normal temperature for a cat is 101 to 102.5°F. Before you call your vet to report a high fever in an Oriental Shorthair cat, think about where that cat was sleeping. Was she on an electric blanket, in the sun, or on top of the heat vent, stove, or microwave?

Since you know how much your cat normally drinks and eats, always watch for changes. Dehydration is a very dangerous sign. To check for this, gently pinch a loose fold of fur and skin between your fingers and drop it. If it doesn't go back to normal within a few seconds, your friend may be dehydrated.

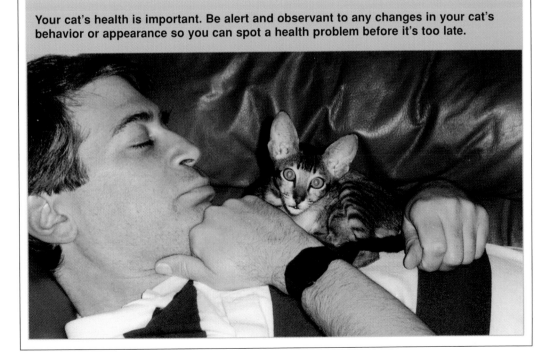

Your cat's health is important. Be alert and observant to any changes in your cat's behavior or appearance so you can spot a health problem before it's too late.

Vets can inject fluids beneath the skin of dehydrated cats and may even teach you how to do this at home.

BASIC ANATOMY

A cat is not that much different from a human being in terms of anatomy. Cats have similar muscles, including cardiac, skeletal, and peristaltic muscles. Most cats have about 244 bones, beginning with the skull and ending with the tail.

SKIN

Skin wounds should be washed and observed. Abscesses form easily, and a vet's care may be needed to prevent further infection. Your cat's skin should be smooth and free of scabs. There should be no bugs or insects when you part the hair to see the skin. *Dermatitis* is fairly common. It may be due to allergies or insect bites. If you see inflamed skin on your cat, consult your vet.

Ringworm is a fungus that is highly contagious to people and other pets. Symptoms range from dandruff to pustules to a large amount of hair loss. A vet's care is needed to eradicate this disease.

Chin acne is fairly common in Oriental breeds. It looks like black crusty patches in the chin area. Usually, switching to a stainless steel bowl (that is washed every day), and washing the chin area frequently will ease the problem.

Allergies are common. Sensitivities include food, contact with certain substances,

Allergies and other skin disorders cause itching, scabs, rashes, and hair loss.

inhalation of particles, fleas, intestinal parasites, and medications. It is important that you work with your vet, observe your cat, and keep good records. Most skin allergies cause itching, scabs, rash, and hair loss.

Pododermatitis is a rare skin disease, but it has been observed in Orientals and Siamese. It usually begins with swollen paw pads, and the cat may have difficulty walking. There is no known cause and no known cure or therapy. Time seems to be the best therapy.

Impetigo is usually seen in young kittens. Skin pustules appear, followed by yellowish crusts. Antibiotics, soaks, and veterinary attention are needed.

EYES

Conjunctivitis is an inflammation of the tissue around the eye. If you pull down the lower eyelid, you will

Conjunctivitis, an infection of the tissue surrounding the eye, is a common ailment in cats. Usually, a prescription medication is needed to clear up this disease.

see red tissue. Usually, a prescription medication is needed to clear up this disease. If it is just a little bit red, you may be able to eliminate it by washing the area often with normal saline. If the third eyelid (haw) is raised, then the cat is having more severe difficulty with her health and should be seen by your vet.

Central retinal degeneration is usually caused by a deficiency of taurine in the diet. Blindness will occur as the disease progresses. It was formerly believed that this was hereditary.

INFECTIOUS DISEASES

Upper respiratory infections are known as URIs. They can range from the common cold to a bacterial infection. Usual symptoms are sneezing, runny eyes, stuffed nose, cough, red eyes, teary eyes, anorexia (loss of appetite), sleeping more than usual, and lack of interest in doing anything. A cat relies on her nose to smell food. If she cannot breathe clearly, she may not want to eat, and force-feeding is necessary. There are good, palatable canned foods to give in this situation, or you can try tempting, strong-smelling goodies like sardines or warm, low-sodium chicken broth. Speak to your vet about this and about mineral supplements that come in a tube. Good hand-washing techniques must be used as well as isolating the sick cat if you have other cats. Your vet may give you antibiotics to prevent secondary infection. Regular over-the-counter saline nose spray may be used in the nostrils to aid breathing. A vaporizer may be set up in the cat's room for severe congestion. If you don't have a vaporizer, the bathroom can be steamed up with hot water from the shower.

Herpesvirus is responsible for *feline viral rhinotracheitis*, one type of URI. The majority of cats from multi-cat households have herpes and may be carriers for life. Most of the time, these cats will be the epitome of health. Suddenly, they will have a flare-up of symptoms. Many vets recommend giving them L-Lysine for a few days until symptoms subside. This amino acid is available at any health food store, and your vet will know the correct dosage for your cat.

Feline calicivirus also causes URIs but is more resistant to treatment than herpes. According

When one cat in a household has an infectious illness, it won't be long before every cat is sick. It's vital to isolate the sick cat for the duration of the illness.

to *The Cornell Book of Cats*, the virus can survive for one or more weeks at room temperature.

Feline infectious peritonitis (FIP) is a severe and usually fatal disease caused by a coronavirus. According to Susan Little, DVM, of the Cat Fanciers' Association Health Committee, "FIP is the term for clinical disease associated with feline coronavirus infection. The common benign form of feline coronavirus is referred to as FECV. FECV (feline enteric coronavirus) is spread primarily by the fecal-oral route and, to a lesser degree, through saliva or respiratory droplets. When FECV has mutated into a disease-causing form, it is then referred to as FIPV (feline infectious peritonitis virus). Feline coronaviruses in general are referred to as FCoV." Inhalation and ingestion seem to be the usual way for the infection to be passed from cat to cat. Effusive

(wet) FIP includes fluid in one or more body cavities. Dry, or non-effusive, FIP is more sudden and severe. Respiratory difficulties, jaundice, anemia, depression, and fever are common symptoms. Diagnosis is not easy and must be made by history, biopsy, and lab tests. Lab tests alone do not make the diagnosis, because high measurements of coronavirus antibody only mean that the cat has been exposed to a related virus. If your vet disagrees, take your cat and run to another vet quickly. *The Cornell Book of Cats* states, "The diagnosis of FIP must never be made simply on the basis of a coronavirus antibody test."

Feline immunodeficiency virus (FIV) is a new virus that has been placed in the same virus family as acquired immunodeficiency syndrome (AIDS). However, it is a different virus that is not transmissible to humans. Secondary infection, anemia, low white blood cell counts, and general failure to thrive are some of the symptoms.

Rabies is an old disease that still occurs in cats. Most states require mandatory rabies vaccines ranging from every year to every three years. These vaccinations are very important even for indoor cats—imagine if a bat flew into your home and bit your unvaccinated cat!

Feline leukemia virus (FeLV) is contagious and may be fatal, although some adult cats will develop immunity. The best way to prevent FeLV is not to allow it into your house. Test all cats coming into the house and test all cats going out of the house. Isolate new cats until you are sure that they do not have the virus. If you are buying a new kitten, insist that the breeder has also followed these rules, and you should not encounter the virus. There are two types of blood tests for FeLV. One is the ELISA test, which may be run in the veterinarian's office. The other is the Hardy or IFA test, which must be sent to a lab. If a cat tests positive with one test, the other test should be performed.

Feline panleukopenia (FPV) is highly contagious and usually fatal. It usually affects kittens and should be prevented with vaccination.

VACCINATIONS

Vaccinations are usually given to kittens starting at about six weeks of age. They usually receive two booster shots three weeks apart. They receive a rabies vaccine (required by law in many states) at about 16 weeks. Often, the breeder will give the vaccines (except rabies) at home, because of health concerns about taking small kittens to the veterinarian's office. A vet who makes housecalls is of great value here, because she can come to examine all of the babies, vaccinate as needed, test those leaving the cattery for FeLV, and check for parasites as needed.

Most breeders do not vaccinate cats for FeLV, because they do not expect their cats to come into contact with FeLV-positive cats. If you are buying a new cat from a breeder, he or she will expect that any cats you already own have

tested negative. Also, because no one has shown that the test and vaccine for FIP actually work, the majority of breeders and veterinarians do not use them.

Feline panleukopenia (FP) vaccination programs differ in different circumstances. Work with your vet to find the best schedule for your cat. Feline viral rhinotracheitis (FVR) is sometimes given in combination with other vaccines. Feline calicivirus (FCV) is usually given in combination. Rabies should be given from once a year to once every three years. Feline leukemia virus (FeLV) vaccine is available but not recommended by all

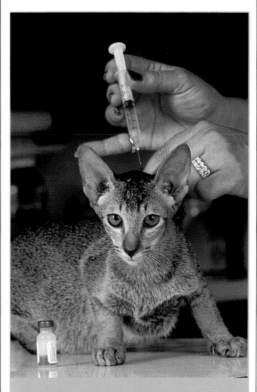

Vaccinations are usually given to kittens starting at about six weeks of age. Even for indoor cats, it's important to vaccinate cats annually after that.

breeders. Feline infectious peritonitis (FIP) vaccine is not recommended until further studies are done.

DIGESTIVE SYSTEM

Vomiting is not pleasant for you or your cat, but most cats do not do it often. Others seem to do it as a form of recreation. Your active Oriental cat may vomit just after eating. Many call this "scarf and barf"—the food may or may not be digested yet. Whether they are just eating too quickly, overeating, or allergic to the food is something to look into. You may want to change brands, feed small meals more often, or report the problem to your vet. While hairballs may be the cause, this is not always the case.

Diarrhea could be caused by illness, overeating, food allergy, parasites, eating an insect, or stress. Diarrhea may be a sign of viral enteritis, bacterial enteritis, dietary problems, poisoning, parasites, and other medical problems that need to be determined by your veterinarian. Observe your cat, and if the diarrhea continues for more than a couple of days, talk to your vet.

Constipation does not occur often in healthy cats. Sometimes a change in food is necessary. Sometimes the cat is not drinking enough water. Try adding water to the canned food. Put extra dishes of water around the house. In the case of an older feline, there may be a medical reason, and medicines and/or enemas may be needed.

The causes of constipation are

usually medical, and the vet will have to diagnose the problem and medicate appropriately.

When not enough insulin is being produced by the pancreas, the result is *diabetes mellitus.* It is most often seen in middle-aged and older cats. It can usually be controlled at home by diet and insulin injections.

URINARY TRACT

Feline lower urinary tract disease (FLUTD) is common. It used to be called FUS or just cystitis. There are many theories about the cause—bacteria, foods, viruses, stress, heredity, and patterns of urination. Urination in inappropriate places is a sign of this disease, as is straining in the litter box. Bloody urine, drinking a lot of water, and returning to the litter box frequently are all signs. Your vet must treat this as the emergency that it is when you call him in the middle of the night.

Pyelonephritis is an infection of the kidney(s). It may be the result of a bladder infection or secondary to an infection elsewhere in the body.

Amyloidosis is diagnosed when the amyloid protein is deposited in the kidneys. The cause is unknown, although it is thought to be inherited.

Chronic renal failure is a disease process in which more than 70 percent of kidney function is already destroyed. The cause may be known, but the cure is not. Treatment consisting of subcutaneous fluids, special diets, and medications as needed should control the progression of the disease. Kidney transplants have been performed successfully in cats in some areas of the US.

REPRODUCTION

Most diseases of the reproductive system in female cats will not occur in young kittens, spayed cats, and cats that have never been pregnant. It is assumed that the majority of readers of this book live with spayed and neutered cats and therefore will not encounter these problems. Some of these are hormone imbalances, infertility, ovarian tumors, infections of the uterus and vagina, and even juvenile mammary enlargement.

Pyometra is an infection of the uterus that may occur at any time in the unspayed female's life. It requires immediate veterinary care. The preferred method of treatment is removal of the uterus (spaying). If a cat is a valuable breeding cat in the eyes of the breeder, medication may be tried.

Mastitis usually occurs in the nursing queen. It is an infection of the mammary glands. She will probably have a high fever and tender, warm, swollen breasts. She will probably not want to eat, nurse, or do anything but lie there feeling awful. A cat with mastitis requires immediate medical care. The vet will probably give her antibiotics and possibly subcutaneous fluids for dehydration. She may need surgical drainage. She will require warm soaks and special care if she starts draining and the area becomes an open wound. You will also have to take care of the babies, as they will not be allowed to nurse but will probably not be old enough to eat on their own.

Some *congenital malformations* include cleft palate, spina bifida, conjoined twins, cardiovascular problems, limb defects, diaphragmatic hernia (opening in the diaphragm that allows abdominal organs to bulge through), gastroschisis (the intestines protrude outside of the body), and cryptorchidism (one or both testicles will not descend into the scrotum). Sometimes the testicles will be underdeveloped, which is called congenital testicular hypoplasia.

Some of the diseases that may occur in unspayed female cats include hormone imbalances, infertility, ovarian tumors, and infections of the uterus, vagina, and mammary glands.

CARDIAC DISEASE

Cardiomyopathy is a disease of the heart. It is usually caused by a deficiency of taurine in the diet, although it may be hereditary in some cats. Although it cannot be cured, it can be controlled for a number of years with various medications. Hypertrophic cardiomyopathy is found in young cats. The signs are labored breathing, lethargy, and sometimes paralysis of the rear legs. Dilated cardiomyopathy is usually found in middle-aged or older cats. Congestive heart failure is common. Years ago, it was discovered that many cases were caused by taurine deficiencies in cat food. Restrictive cardiomyopathy usually occurs in older cats.

CANCER

Tumors may be found in any area of a cat's body. Cancer treatment has come a long way in recent years, and veterinary oncologists have saved many felines with chemotherapy, surgery, and radiation. Some common tumors are basal cell and squamous cell, papilloma, fibrosarcoma, mast cell, cutaneous, melanoma, liposarcoma, lymphosarcoma and hemangioma. Most skin tumors require surgery. Squamous cell carcinoma in the mouth usually responds to radiation therapy.

HEALTH CONCERNS OF ORIENTALS

There are probably no more major health concerns in the Oriental Shorthair than in other breeds. Over the past few years, Oriental Shorthair breeders have been among the most verbal in talking about their cats with lymphosarcoma. All of the affected cats have been FeLV-negative, and vets all over the country have been surprised by the diagnoses and the young age at which they are diagnosed. Early diagnosis and immediate treatment seem to be the key in remission of this disease. Many Oriental Shorthairs have completed two years of chemotherapy treatments and continue to do well. There is a support group on the Internet that started out as mostly Oriental Shorthair and Colorpoint Shorthair owners whose cats had lymphosarcoma but now represents many breeds and age groups, with cats from every corner of the world.

PARASITES

There are many organisms that can afflict your cat. Roundworm, tapeworm, hookworm, coccidia, and giardia are just some of them. They are diagnosable and treatable. Some external parasites are fleas, ticks, mites, and flies. There are now some internal and external medications for these parasites available from your vet.

There are many kinds of intestinal parasites. None of them is good for your cat. Watch for them in the litter box, test your cat's feces, and keep the litter box clean. Always wash your hands after changing the litter box. Intestinal parasites are all curable, although repeat treatments are not unusual.

Ear mites are common in kittens and adults and are contagious between cats and dogs. To the naked eye, the inside of the ear looks dirty with brown material. The cat may scratch frequently and shake her head. The vet looks at the brown material under the microscope and sees the mites, which look like tiny spiders. Treatment with ear drops is easy.

Fleas are very common, small, powerful jumpers without wings. They can cause severe anemia in young kittens and major skin problems in older cats. The environment as well as the cat needs to be treated. Several new products on the market are available through your veterinarian, making flea treatment much easier than it was in the past.

Examine your cat's ears regularly for the telltale sign of ear mites—copious, dirty-looking earwax.

RECOMMENDED READING

Every cat owner should have reference books available to him or her day and night. Without some of my favorite cat health books, I would not have been able to care for my cats appropriately. Sexing kittens, tube feeding, illness, symptoms, and treatments are just some of the things I learned in my books. My favorites are *Robinson's Genetics for Cat Breeders & Veterinarians* by Carolyn M. Vella, Lorraine M. Shelton, John J. McGonagle, Jr., and Terry W. Stanglein, VMD; *The Cornell Book of Cats,* edited by Mordecai Siegal; and *The Well Cat Book,* by Terri McGinnis, DVM.

GROOMING

Orientals love to be handled by the people they live with, their friends, relatives, and anyone else who happens to visit. Most of them enjoy being at shows and playing with the judges too.

Whether your cat is staying home or going to a show, grooming is pretty easy. I usually begin with clipping the claws. This should be done about once a week. Your cat will let you know when it's time when he jumps onto your shoulder and you feel 18 little claws in your back. I use a small scissors-type, stainless steel nail clipper that is inexpensive in pet stores, catalogs, or at cat shows. Just clip the tips

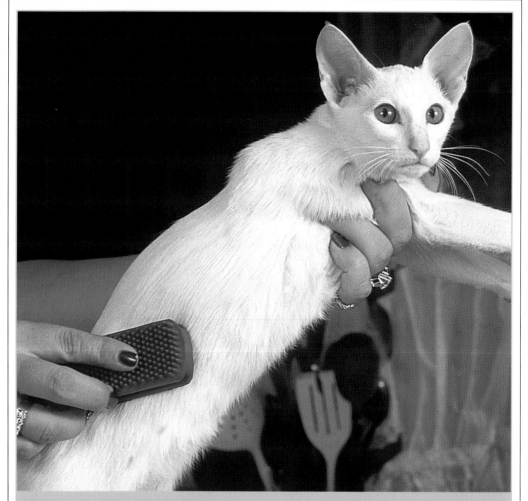

A rubber brush with a flat side and a curved side is the best tool for grooming an Oriental Shorthair.

and beware of the red line on the claws—a living vein called the "quick." Clean the eyes with a moist cotton ball. Clean the ears with a different moist cotton ball. Brush your cat regularly. My favorite tool is a rubber brush with a flat side and a curved side. There are other brushes that can be used but be careful not to strip out the undercoat if you are going to show your cat. To finish, just wipe your hands, a chamois cloth, or a silk scarf over the entire coat.

If you are grooming your cat at a show, you will be finished while the Maine Coon exhibitor next to you is still assembling all of the necessary grooming tools she will need. There are shampoos, coat sprays, powders, combs, grooming tools, and more that some Oriental exhibitors use. Some will shave the hair on the inside of the ears and some will not. Judges can tell how big the cat's ears are with or without the hair, but some prefer one look or the other.

LINKS TO CAT HEALTH WEB SITES

There are countless resources on the Internet for cat lovers. These are some of the best health sites, and while they were correct at press time, Web addresses do change. Check a search engine for the latest addresses.

A Diagnostic Support System for Veterinary Medicine
www.vet.cornell.edu/consultant/consult.asp

Feline Chronic Renal Failure
www.best.com/~lynxpt/

Good Source of Information About Feline Lymphosarcoma
www.ferretcentral.org/faq/med/lymph.html#treatment

Personal History of Cases of Feline Lymphosarcoma
members.home.net/victorsm/Feline_Lymphosarcoma.html

Lymphosarcoma at University of Pennsylvania
cancer.med.upenn.edu/specialty/vet_onc/treat/cat_lsa.html

Veterinary Cancers at University of Pennsylvania
cancer.med.upenn.edu/specialty/vet_onc/general/vet_treat.html

Lymphosarcoma at UP— Treatment Options
cancer.med.upenn.edu/specialty/vet_onc/treat/cat_lsa.html

Veterinary Chemotherapy at University of Pennsylvania
cancer.med.upenn.edu/specialty/vet_onc/general/vet_treat.html

Great Articles About All Aspects of Cat Care
www.fabcats.org

Tumor Information
www.gulfcoastvetspec.com/Oncology/gcvo_tumorinfo.htm

American Veterinary Medical Assoc. presents animal health and more
www.avma.org/care4pets/default.htm

How to Select a Veterinarian
www.avma.org/care4pets/othrselv.htm

What You Need to Know About FeLV
www.priory.co.uk/vet/feleuv01.htm

Fighting FeLV
www.bright.net/~zimm1/FightingFeLV/

What To Do if Your Cat Tests Positive
www.bright.net/~zimm1/FightingFeLV/

Feline Leukemia FAQ
www2.dgsys.com/~ermiller/FeLV.html

Feline Behavior Problems
www.vet.cornell.edu/Public/FHC/behav.html

Feline Vaccinations
www.vet.cornell.edu/Public/FHC/vaccbr.html

Diabetes in Cats
www.vet.cornell.edu/Public/FHC/diabetes.html

Feline Lower Urinary Tract Disease
www.vet.cornell.edu/Public/FHC/urinary.html

Inflammatory Bowel Disease
www.vet.cornell.edu/Public/FHC/ibd.html

Toxoplasmosis in Cats
www.vet.cornell.edu/Public/FHC/toxo.html

Feline Immunodeficiency Virus (FIV)
www.vet.cornell.edu/Public/FHC/fiv.html

The Association for Pet Loss and Bereavement
www.aplb.org/frameset4.htm

Cornell Pet Loss Support Hotline
web.vet.cornell.edu/Public/petloss/index.htm

The Facts about Euthanasia
web.vet.cornell.edu/Public/petloss/saeuth.htm

EXHIBITING YOUR ORIENTAL SHORTHAIR

Cat shows are fun to visit all over the world. The way that cats are shown is unique in different geographical areas and various associations.

The standard show in the US consists of 6 to 12 rings, with different judges in each ring. Most shows are held over a weekend. The exhibitor brings her cats to the ring. Spectators and exhibitors are welcome to sit in the chairs in front of the rings and observe. Many judges will talk about the qualities that they are looking for in a breed.

In England, a standard format is for the cat to be set up in an unmarked cage. The exhibitors leave the show hall. The judge and steward travel among the cages with a rolling cart. When the exhibitors and spectators are invited to return, the cats have already been judged.

The most up-to-date means of finding a cat show in a specific organization is to visit their Web site. Some associations have a special Web site for show calendars, which are listed in the box at right.

Judges at American cat shows will often talk about the qualities that they are looking for in a breed. Here, GP Lokikats Santeria, a chestnut silver tabby, is being evaluated.

SHOWING YOUR ORIENTAL— UNITED STATES STYLE

Exhibiting your cat at a cat show can be so much fun. You can show as an individual or bring the family for a learning experience for all. Just think about spending two whole days with other cat fanciers!

How to Enter

Once you find the show that you would like to enter, you need to find an entry form. If you visit the association's Web site, you can usually find one there. If not, contact the entry clerk. Be sure to address the envelope to the entry clerk, write the check to the cat club, complete the entry form and send a short note

CAT SHOW CALENDARS ONLINE

American Association of Cat Enthusiasts (AACE) Show Schedule
www.aaceinc.org/showsch.htm
American Cat Fanciers Association (ACFA) Show Schedule
www.acfacat.com/calendar.htm
Australian Cat Federation (ACF) Show Schedule
www.acf.asn.au/infoshowdate.html
Canadian Cat Association/ Association Feline Canadienne Show Schedule
www.cca-afc.com/shows.html
Cat Fanciers' Association (CFA) Show Schedule
www.cfainc.org/shows/show-schedule.html
Cat Fanciers Federation (CFF) Show Schedule
www.cffinc.org/shows.html
Cat Federation of Southern Africa (CFSA) Show Schedule
www.cfsa.co.za/showreg/calendar.htm
European Show Schedule
www.dataweb.net/~sham/show2.html
Feline Control Council of Victoria, Australia (FCCV) Show Schedule
www.hotkey.net.au/~fccvic/fccv4.htm
Governing Council of the Cat Fancy (GCCF) Show Schedule
ourworld.compuserve.com/homepages/ GCCF_CATS/shows.htm
The International Cat Association (TICA) Show Schedule
www.tica.org/catshows.htm

saying that this is your first show. Some clubs will help you, and some will not. When you know which association(s) you will be showing in, buy a copy of the show rules. You will need them to help you complete the entry forms.

Unless your cat is a Household Pet (meaning that she is not registered as a purebred), you will also need her registration number. If your cat is a kitten, you do not need the number to enter her, but it's a good idea to register the kitten so you can give the number at the check-in table for the show.

Some shows are very popular and close months ahead of the show date, so plan in advance. Other shows can still be entered one weekend before the show. Contact the entry clerk for more information.

Which Shows to Enter?

When you go to shows, you will hear about other shows. You will also receive a mountain of flyers throughout the weekend. Sort through them at the show hall or bring them all home. Remember that exhibitors who are campaigning their cat for a championship go to shows every weekend and may be interested in going to a show 3,000 miles from home. Chances are, you will not be willing to travel that far.

Cats Magazine, Cat Fancy, CFA Almanac, and *TICA Trend* have listings, but not all shows are listed in any of them. Remember that they go to print at least two months prior to the time they arrive in your mailbox.

On the Internet, you will find shows listed on the association's Web site. This is the best place to look for a show, because it is usually more up-to-date than the publications and usually has e-mail addresses, phone, and fax numbers that you will need for more information.

What to Bring to the Show

Directions, maps, a cell phone, and road service plans are very handy when showing. The club will send you directions to the show hall, which may or may not be correct. Don't take a chance. Get your own through Internet mapping sites. These may or may not be correct either, but you will at least have a choice as to which way to go.

A wheeled luggage cart is the easiest way to get your stuff into the show hall unless there are steps. It will hold your bags and your cat's carrier. It will also help hold all of the things that you purchase during the show.

Your cat(s) should already be groomed, with front and back claws trimmed short, ears shaved if they will be shaved, eyes clean, ears clean—almost ready to be judged.

You will need cage curtains, a sheet, material, or something else to cover the cage top, sides, and bottom. Most cages in the US are 22" by 22" by 22". Most exhibitors splurge for a double cage, which gives you 22" of additional space across. It also gives you space for more "stuff" under the cage, as well as two chairs instead of one.

You should also bring thesis clips to hold cage curtains, repair the cage as needed, hang toys, hold the trash bag, etc. You can never have too many of them. Bring a water dish, food dish, favorite food, or baby food. Utensils and a can opener are always useful.

Also bring a litter box that is small enough to fit in the cage. Collapsible, disposable cardboard boxes are the easiest to travel with. I use an inexpensive disposable roasting pan.

Grooming supplies may include chamois, silk scarf, rubber brush, cotton balls, cotton swabs, claw clippers, special grooming paraphernalia, sprays, potions, and even good luck charms.

GC Kattalyst's Kattalina Myst and her brother, GP Kattalyst Beautiful Stranger, demonstrate a typical cage setup at an American show.

Remember that Orientals do not really require a lot of grooming. Bring whatever makes you feel like you are doing something, especially if you are benched next to a Maine Coon or Persian exhibitor who spends the whole day grooming her cat.

Bring a copy of the cat's registration certificate and rabies certificate. I like to copy them onto one piece of paper. Compare the registration number with the number printed in the show catalog. If they are different, speak to the master clerk who will help you with a catalog correction.

Don't forget snack food, lunch, coffee, cups, plates, utensils, and whatever else you think that you may need. There is always "people food" for sale. It can range from hot dogs to home-cooked meals to expensive-but-not-worth-it sandwiches or salads. Once you are showing for a while, you will decide with your friends whether to bring food and have a potluck or send someone out to the local hamburger, pizza, or chicken place that you passed on the way to the show hall.

Tips

Bring bottled water for you and your cat. Check the judging schedule, listen for changes, listen for numbers called to rings, and check rings for numbers. Microphones are not always audible. Judging schedules will change throughout the day. Some associations do not announce final numbers. They will say, for example, "The

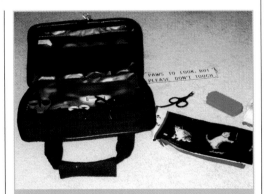

This grooming bag is all packed and ready for a cat show. Nail clippers, a rubber brush, a silk scarf, a glove, a cage sign, and many other essential items are included.

numbers are posted for the premiership final in Ring Three."

When your cat is in a final and he is called to another ring, quietly go to that ring and tell the clerk that your cat is in a final. When you must rush to a ring for judging or a final and you are coming from a final, be discreet with the rosette. Leave it at your cage, with a friend, or on a chair with your catalog in the spectator section before bringing your cat to a ring.

It is proper show etiquette to stay in the show hall until the advertised closing time. Most exhibitors will stay past that time if judging is still going on.

SHOWING YOUR ORIENTAL— GCCF STYLE

Cat shows licensed by the Governing Council of the Cat Fancy (GCCF) in England are closely governed by rules for the protection of both exhibitors and exhibits. It is therefore essential for every exhibitor to buy a copy

One way to display all the rosettes that you and your cat win at shows is to hang them on a strip used for edging carpets.

of the GCCF rules before entering a show.

All official GCCF publications are available for sale from the GCCF office (see contact information in the Associations chapter). As well as the rules, these include the constitution, standards of points, list of breed numbers, stud books, show list, list of affiliated clubs, list of judges, and list of club welfare officers.

Pedigreed cats must be registered with the GCCF at least three weeks before they are shown, and if they have been transferred, this must also have taken place at least three weeks before the show. Applications for registrations, transfers, certified pedigrees, or prefixes must be sent to the office. Cats registered with the GCCF may never be shown at non-GCCF shows without special permission.

The most important shows are championship shows. All-breed championship shows cover every pedigreed breed that is recognized by the GCCF: each breed that has full or provisional recognition has its own open class while breeds that only have preliminary recognition may be seen in assessment classes. There are also specialist championship shows that cover a single breed or group of breeds.

Entering a Show

Before you can enter a show, you will need a schedule and entry form. The GCCF show list gives names and addresses of show managers to whom you should send a stamped addressed envelope with your request for a schedule. When you receive the schedule, study it carefully, and decide which classes your cat is eligible to enter.

Show standards at championship shows are extremely high, so do study your standard of points carefully before you decide to exhibit. If a cat or kitten is obviously only "pet type," it is a waste of time and money entering a top show and can only lead to disappointment.

Vetting In

All cats and kittens must have completed a course of vaccination against feline infectious enteritis, feline viral rhinotracheitis and feline calicivirus ("cat flu") and have their booster vaccinations up to date before being shown. Vaccinations must have been given by a veterinary surgeon at least one week before the date of the show. Take your vaccination certificate to the show with you. The GCCF does not accept "homoeopathic vaccinations" for show purposes.

All cats are examined by a veterinary surgeon before being allowed into a show and if they are not perfectly healthy they are liable to be rejected. Any exhibitor whose cat is rejected from a show will receive a rejection form—read this carefully. There are four sections under which a cat may be rejected: Section A covers such reason as fleas, wounds, cats showing signs of having been given drugs, pregnancy, lactation, absence of two testicles in the scrotum in an adult male, poor condition or undersize, distressed cats, or cats that cannot be handled at vetting in. Section B is for cats rejected for ear mites or dirty ears, Section C covers cats that show signs of infectious diseases, and Section D is for cats rejected for skin lesions that might be due to ringworm.

Procedure During the Show

You may be sent your "tally" or you may collect it at the entrance to the show on the day itself. The tally is a disc with your cat's pen number on it. The tally should be hung round the cat's neck with narrow white tape, ribbon or elastic. Many shows permit you to hang the tally on the front of the pen instead, but it should be available to be put around the cat's neck if necessary.

Disinfect the pen with a suitable disinfectant and make certain that the pen is secure. Read the schedule and the GCCF rules very thoroughly and abide by them. Only plain white blankets or white vetbed-type material with a green or white backing are allowed, which means that lacy blankets or fur fabric will lead to disqualification.

Drinking water, in a white container, must always be provided, but food must not be left in the pen during judging. Cats and kittens may be fed at lunchtime. The litter tray must also be white although you can use whichever litter the cat is accustomed to.

Do not stand near your pen while your cat is being judged; this is embarrassing to the judge and stewards and may lead to disqualification. If you wish to consult a judge, wait until he or she has finished all classes and then ask your questions.

(The section *Showing Your Oriental—GCCF Style* was reprinted with the permission of Claire Bessant, Feline Advisory Bureau. For more information, contact the Feline Advisory Bureau: "Taeselbury," High Street, Tisbury, Wiltshire, SP3 6LD, UK; Tel: +44(0)1747 871872; Fax: +44(0)1747 871873; E-mail: fab@fabcats.org; *www.fabcats.org*)

ORIENTALS ONLINE

There are several places to join with other Oriental owners, breeders, and exhibitors. If you are a breeder, you will probably want to be involved with the breed councils or breed groups in your association. But with all of the clubs and breed groups, the place where most Oriental owners probably meet is online. We talk to people all over the world, and it's a wonderful place to share information quickly and easily. There is even an Oriental e-mail list where everything about Orientals can and will be discussed. Whether it is grooming, foods, fun, illness, a rescue cat who needs help, or information about shows—there's always something to talk about. To subscribe, e-mail *orientals-request@fanciers.com, orientals-subscribe@onelist.com* [UK and European fanciers], *siamese-oriental-subscribe@onelist.com* [Dutch and English languages], or *so-grupp@onelist.com* [Swedish language]. There are also several private lists that you may subscribe to if you are a member of a particular club or breed council. For pedigree information, you may want to join *shlinechasers@petplanet.nl.* (Again, please note that all of the instructions and addresses were correct as of press time.)

The Fanciers list is a huge list with high volume and is not for everyone. Anything about the cat fancy can and will be discussed here. The list began in 1993 and has grown to more than 850 members. Their Web site is filled with information and links to other sites. Visit them at *www.fanciers.com.*

One online term used often is *FAQ,* which means Frequently Asked Questions. If you see an FAQ about any topic, it should answer your questions before you have a chance to ask them. Several Oriental breeders around the country wrote the Oriental Shorthair/Oriental Longhair FAQ several years ago. Visit it at *members.home.net/victorsm/ osh-faq.html*

There is a wonderful collection of Oriental, Siamese, and Colorpoint Shorthair information by Cheryl and Tony Classick. It can be found at The Oriental Shorthair/ Colorpoint Shorthair Home Page: *w3.one.net/~arazi/welcome1.html.* If you want to see different colors of Orientals, visit "A Kaleidoscope of Colors—The Oriental Shorthair" at *w3.one.net/~arazi/kaleid.html.*

There are several cat clubs for Orientals. Oriental Shorthairs of America is one of the largest CFA clubs and invites new members to join. The Web address is *www.geocities.com/Heartland/ Woods/4291.* Webmasters Julie and Roy Keyer have assembled many photographs of Orientals, great links, and a fun page to visit.

On America Online, there are message boards for every breed, including Orientals. There are also chats about pedigreed cats and cat shows. You can find these by doing a search. Prodigy and CompuServe have their own pet message boards.

Finding Oriental Breeders Online

Locating Oriental breeders online is very easy. Fanciers' Breeder Referral List has three sections:

Oriental Longhair Breeders: *www.breedlist.com/oriental-lh-breeders.html*

Oriental Shorthair Breeders—US: *www.breedlist.com/oriental-sh-breeders.html*

Oriental Shorthair Breeders Worldwide: *www.breedlist.com/wor/oris-wor.html*

Mailing Lists

There are many other cat-related e-mail lists around the world. The following is part of a list that Mimi Sluiter has coordinated. She has given permission to share this with you.
ACFA [USA]: *ACFA@petplanet.nl*
Canada [General]: *canadiancats@onelist.com*
CCA [Canada]: *CCAcats@onelist.com*
CFA [USA/Europe/Japan]: *CFA-list@ fanciers.com*
Europe [General]: *eurofanciers@petplanet.nl*
FIFe [Europe/Asia/South America]: *fife@petplanet.nl*
France: *chats@onelist.com* [French language]
Germany/Austria/Switzerland [General]: *katzenwelt@petplanet.nl* [German language]
Netherlands [General]: *hollandfanciers@onelist.com* [Dutch language]
New Zealand [General]: *Nzcats @onelist.com*
South Africa [General]: *Sacats@onelist.com* [South African

Whether via e-mail or on the Web, it's fun to talk about your playful, wonderful cats with other fanciers of the breed.

and English language]
South America [General]: *sudamericats@onelist.com* [Spanish language]
TICA [USA/Europe]: *TICA@ fanciers.com,* *TICAcats_list@onelist.com* [German]

Cat Health Lists

Asthma: *felineasthma@onelist.com*
Cancer: *feline_cancer@onelist.com,* *feline_lymphoma@onelist.com*
Chronic Renal Failure: *feline-crf@lists.colorado.edu*
Diabetes: *felinediabetes@onelist.com*
FIP: *FIP@onelist.com,* *FIPsupport-group@onelist.com*
FIV: *FIVcats@onelist.com*
FELV: *felvmed@onelist.com*
General Health: *feline-health@mylist.net,* *vetmed-L@listserv.iupui.edu*

Grooming: *grooming@onelist.com*
Hand-Rearing Kittens:
handrearing@onelist.com
Non-Allopathic Health:
holisticat@mylist.net
Pancreatitis:
pancreatitisincats@onelist.com
PKD: *PKD-list@petplanet.nl, feline-PKD@onelist.com*

How to Subscribe

All addresses given above are those you mail to, once you have become a subscriber. To get on a specific list first, follow the subscribing directions below per server/system that is used.

Lists ending at: fanciers.com: send e-mail to: *majordomo@fanciers.com.* Write in the text field: subscribe *name-of-the-list.*

Lists ending at: lists.colorado.edu: send e-mail to: *listproc@lists.colorado.edu.* Write in the text field: subscribe *name-of-the-list your-name.*

Lists ending at: listserv.iupui.edu: send e-mail to: *listserve@listserv.iupui.edu.* Write in the text field: subscribe *name-of-the-list your-name.*

Lists ending at: mylist.net: send e-mail to: *majordomo@mylist.net.* Write in the text field: subscribe *name-of-the-list.*

Lists ending at: onelist.com: send e-mail to: *listname-subscribe@onelist.com*

Lists ending at: petplanet.nl: send e-mail to: *majordomo@petplanet.nl.* Write in the text field: subscribe *name-of-the-list.*

Interacting with other cat lovers all over the world will open up a new way of looking at everything for you. Have fun visiting, but don't forget to come home to pet your cat.

Interacting with other cat lovers all over the world is wonderful—but don't forget to come home from your "visits" to pet your cat.

CAT REGISTRY ASSOCIATIONS

**American Association
of Cat Enthusiasts**
P.O. Box 213
Pine Brook, NJ 07058
Phone: 973-335-6717
Fax: 973-334-5834
E-mail: info@aaceinc.org
Web: *www.aaceinc.org/
welcome.html*

**American Cat Fanciers
Association**
P.O. Box 203
Point Lookout, MO
65726
Phone: (417) 334-5430
Fax: (417) 334-5540
E-mail: info@acfacat.com
Web: *acfacat.com*

Australian Cat Federation (Inc)
Post Office Box 3305
Port Adelaide SA
5015
Phone: 08 8449 5880
Fax: 08 8242 2767
E-mail: acf@catlover.com
Web: *www.acf.asn.au*

Canadian Cat Association
220 Advance Blvd,
Suite 101
Brampton, Ontario
Canada L6T 4J5
Phone: (905) 459-1481
Fax: (905) 459-4023
E-mail: office@cca-afc.com
Web: *www.cca-afc.com*

**The Cat Fanciers'
Association, Inc.**
P.O. Box 1005
Manasquan, NJ
08736-0805
Phone: (732) 528-9797
Fax: (732) 528-7391
E-mail: cfa@cfainc.org
Web: *www.cfainc.org*

Cat Fanciers Federation
P.O. Box 661
Gratis, OH 45330
Phone: 937-787-9009
Fax: 937-787-4290
E-mail: cff@siscom.net
Web: *www.cffinc.org*

**Cat Federation
of Southern Africa**
P.O. Box 25
Bromhof 2125
Rep. of South Africa
Phone or Fax: +27 11
867-4318
E-mail: webmaster@
cfsa.co.za
Web: *www.cfsa.co.za*

**Federation
Internationale Feline**
Ms. Penelope Bydlinski
Little Dene
Lenham Heath
Maidstone, Kent
GB-ME17 2BS
Phone: +44 1622 850913
Fax: +44 1622 850908
E-mail: penbyd@
compuserve.com
Web: *www.fife.org*

**Federazione Italiana
Associazioni Feline**
c/o Rag. Cesare Ghisi
Via Carlo Poma n.20
46100—Mantova
Phone: 0376-224600
Fax: 0376-224041
E-mail: fiafmn@mynet.it
Web: *www.zero.it/fiaf*

**The Feline Control
Council of Victoria, Inc.**
Royal Melbourne
Showgrounds
Epsom Road
Ascot Vale,
Victoria 3032, Australia
Phone: (03) 9281 7404
Fax: (03) 9376 2973

E-mail: m.jones@
rasv.metbourne.net
Web: *www.hotkey.net.au/
~fccvic*

**Governing Council
of the Cat Fancy**
4-6 Penel Orlieu
Bridgwater, Somerset,
TA6 3PG. (UK)
Phone: +44 (0)
1278 427 575
E-mail: GCCF_CATS@
compuserve.com
Web: *ourworld.
compuserve.com/
homepages/GCCF_CATS/
welcome.htm#office*

**International
Cat Exhibitors, Inc.**
P.O. Box 772424
Coral Springs, FL
33077-2424
Web: *members.aol.com/
jhagercat/ICE.htm*

**The International Cat
Association, Inc.**
P.O. Box 2684
Harlingen, TX 78551
Phone: 956-428-8047
Fax: 956-428-8047
E-mail: ticaeoe@
xanadu2.net
Web: *http://www.tica.org*

United Feline Organization
218 NW 180th Street
Newberry, FL 32669
Phone and fax: 352-
472-3253
Email: UFO1FL@
worldnet.att.net
Web: *www.aracnet.com/
~ltdltd/ufo.htm*

World Cat Federation
Hubertstraße 280
D-45307 Essen, Germany
Phone: +49 201/555724
Fax: +49 201/509040
E-mail: wcf@nrw-online.de
Web: *home.nrw-online.de/
wcf/english/ehome.html*

INDEX